The Down Jacket Syndrome

A Successful Business...Not

by

Sara Klepe

DORRANCE PUBLISHING CO., INC.
PITTSBURGH, PENNSYLVANIA 15222

All Rights Reserved
Copyright © 1998 by Sara Klepe
No part of this book may be reproduced or transmitted
in any form or by any means, electronic or mechanical,
including photocopying, recording, or by any information
storage and retrieval system without permission in
writing from the publisher.

ISBN # 0-8059-4224-6
Printed in the United States of America

First Printing

For information or to order additional books, please write:
Dorrance Publishing Co., Inc.
643 Smithfield Street
Pittsburgh, Pennsylvania 15222
U.S.A.

Dedication

To retail entrepreneurs everywhere

WAYNE,

Contents

Part Two

Foreword

Did you ever hear the quip, "That's retail business for you?" It really covers a lot of territory–good aspects and bad–of that unique form of doing business in today's world of commerce. The retail business is never the same from year to year, even month to month, or week to week. I'm no "pro," only an entrepreneur who gave it a whirl for almost three years. I'll never be the same again, nor would I have missed it for anything.

What motivated me, a woman forty years away from my meager retail experience, to compete in our fast–paced world again? I considered pros and cons, an equal number of each, incidentally. I was ready for a change from volunteer to paid work, I liked a specialty store idea, and the time was now or never.

Reasons against: feet problems, merchandise buying inexperience, compatibility with owner (husband) may deteriorate, and physically and mentally adjusting to two jobs. My husband's early retirement might be earlier if I were successful, and we could both be active in the business. Experienced people were available to give input, and financial risk seemed not too large. And so we took the plunge.

All names have been changed to protect the innocent and guilty in this true story.

I now consider my experience a college education in marketing, human relations, economics, psychology, social problems, salesmanship, counseling, bookkeeping, taxation, and survival of the fittest. That you may be a better informed consumer and entrepreneur is my wish.

Sara Klepe

Setting the Scene

The following is from a letter written by me, the author-manager, to distant friends not likely to see my dream come true.

"Girls, this retail clerk of forty years ago has decided to manage a large factory outlet of men's, women's, and children's clothes. I tend to think I must have wanted to die earlier than necessary and some of the reasons are these:

"I spent months painting floors and walls, staining and varnishing fixtures, planning, buying clothes; sleepless hours deciding, wondering ad infinitum, to experience the following.

"The month of July, working day and night checking goods of which every shipment had an error, or the help thought there was an error. Taking my time to recheck, finding we were wrong was embarrassing. Every radio station wanted ad business, every newspaper also; store supplies are something else.

"Books, hooks, signs, calculator, cleaning supplies, hangers (four kinds), bags, marking guns, tags, file, furniture, steamer, lights increased, fitting rooms mirrored, show window railed off from kids who like scarecrows, play stools with books and crayons for them. The cash register decided not to tally tax after arriving home, forty miles from its seller. We reprogrammed that computerized machine twice by phone.

"Since nothing goes as planned, or as smoothly, I'm not surprised that rack size-rings came late, our name-printed balloons for the grand opening were canceled by the company we ordered them from, the telephone company left our store name off the Information list, the newspaper photographer came a day early, omitting the photo of the assistant manager, while an employee swept dust and plaster from the electrician's installations on opening day. Dun & Bradstreet wanted our store registration as of now, which my accountant (husband) wanted to handle. When we were ready to relax, a radio station manager desired ad material."

The store of 2400 square feet, located in the lower level of a downtown mall, was half-carpeted; the other half had a painted floor. Our son-in-law, Brad, constructed the racks, shelves, benches, wagons, and the tables for a children's play area with a country store decor, which was fun to plan. I quickly stained them a dark shade. The wagon wheels and two wheel racks were accented with a turquoise color. The counter was dark paneled with a smooth light wood for the top.

The two outer walls were shelf-lined most of the way. Half the back wall contained three women's fitting rooms. One fitting room for the men's department was next to the show window on the front wall, near the play area. By the front eight-foot entrance to the mall's hall, sealed by a heavy chain mesh door, the cash register set on the counter near the wall phone.

The office and storage were in the back room. Racks of clothes filled the store itself, while two large wagons held items like underwear, socks, or infant wear.

We had set aside an amount of money to use for the business: the cost of the store lease, utilities, stocking it with merchandise, insurance, wages, taxes, fixtures, supplies, and other overhead costs. Included was the primary assurance for we neophytes: hiring an advisor in the retail business. My husband Charles found Al, who had owned a few stores and now worked as a business broker and Realtor. Kent, a young, experienced, unmarried man who worked evenings elsewhere as a security guard, was hired as assistant manager under me. I felt good with him in charge of the men's department.

Our daughter Lisa, my assistant as buyer and part-time saleswoman, also did alterations, being a professional seamstress. Brad, her husband, a sign-maker and advertiser elsewhere, helped greatly. Kim, another daughter, liked the idea of part-time saleswoman, a break from her four young ones at home. The only regular saleslady was Tanya. Angela, also experienced, was added much later. The prime salesman I dealt with was Mike Dida; the prime thief was Mickey Page, whom Detective Parks later investigated.

Three scarecrows (racks), whose skinny stick-arms held lightweight clothes, were placed about the store.

John, with a typical round face and wide-eyed look, wore a straw hat, torn jeans, and a frayed green sweater. He stood in the show window facing the mall elevator, stairway, and hall.

Cecil, a twin, better dressed in a neat straw hat, old dress shirt, and gray pants, eyed the men's section and play area.

Elsie, with a decorated straw beach hat from which her straw hair hung, wore blue slacks and a printed brown sweater with a peach scarf. She smiled down at the women's and children's departments.

Our oldest granddaughter helped dress and name the scarecrows, which served two purposes: answering kids' questions and designating which one would carry what items.

Mannequin Alexandra, a shapely brunette beauty, was later added to a second show window for contrast.

Opening Grandly

Everyone likes a grand opening, don't they? Before holding ours, we had been in business for a week to eliminate some kinks of our great enterprise. Big banners hung across the store and show window. Now was the week of the public celebration, with door prizes, drawings, promotions, and an opening sale. Charles and Al, our authorities, wanted the grand opening earlier, but we girls said we couldn't be ready for the extra work it involved. We differed rather strongly, but all was smoothed over and Al even sent a yucca tree for its opening.

The specials were some cute kids' bedspreads, spice racks, plaid stadium blankets, and matching luggage for the adults, bought at a discount. There were clothes for each department, too. And the grand drawing prize was a stereo. Every customer signed tickets for the prizes.

I planned to use names from the drawing for my mailing list for sale flyers. We hired an extra girl to help on the floor; this was just like big time, you know. It meant lots of advertising to reach the whole area, since this was the first outlet store in town–an unfamiliar concept. People asked if we sold used clothes, seconds, or inferior goods; they didn't understand what promos, close-outs, salesmen's samples, and overstocks meant. That's retail for you: Use the same methods or confuse people, I suppose.

Our balloon promoter was a dud! I had visions of balloons floating to the ceiling, up the stairs, and carried through the mall by the little ones with our store name for all to see. But that company canceled my order. Why? The stickers I put on the kids instead just didn't do the trick.

When the week was over, the drawings began. Can't say we made a big splash in the mall, though we tried. Tanya drew the winning tickets and I notified all winners to come and collect their prizes. Charles wanted a promotion picture of the young girl who won the grand prize, but he couldn't be there when she came for the stereo. It sure was fun, whatever the results. So much for opening grandly!

The Advisor

Initially, do most women business managers need a man's input? That depends: Al, the advisor for ours, planned this country store, wood-looks, and ordered designs for it, including display window and logo. He researched the location and names for it and its needs. Other spots he had in mind were outside the mall.

We considered where the most traffic flowed by: on the freeway coming into town, in three business districts in the suburbs, and even next door to an adults only theater. What was wrong with that? Parents might not want their kids shopping so close to it, or it might also hurt the store's reputation, or could have done the opposite, alerting all where it was.

Finding a name wasn't easy either. Al advised, "It can't be like any other in the state. I'll check, unless it's so far away no one would be confused." The first one picked, The Corral, was changed for that reason. Same with a logo for advertising: a scarecrow was chosen.

Al also helped find names of suppliers and went on a few buying trips with us. He showed us other factory outlets in the state, introduced us to the owners to discuss sources of clothes, the amount of markup and markdown compared to the typical retail stores. He advised us on the prizes for the drawings during grand opening.

There was much to learn and it cost a mint, so we wanted to do it right. Al and Charles took Lisa and me to order down jackets for men and women—our biggest order, which took a lot of storage room because they're so puffy. We thought the men ordered too many which shrank our stock budget. We shopped for women's and children's items, also at the garment shows at the Capitol Civic Center. More fun. We met some salesmen (representatives) who offered samples of sweaters and coordinates that were beautiful. The men's department got expensive sample blazers made in Europe. The few irregulars were in the men's underwear, pants, and all the jeans. We had to find new sources, thinking ahead all the time.

Now Al hadn't sold clothes, just other commodities, but he did tell us how to price, and said, "To keystone means doubling what you paid for it, the usual practice. Mark it down for sales and still make a profit. The trick is to buy lower than the others. Do not buy lines people haven't heard of here." I checked labels in the better stores to find their reps' names in the list published by the Retail Association.

Al advised where to set the racks and arrange the goods. "Remember to put the highest racks in the back so the lower ones can be seen; small sizes go on the rack front. Everything is arranged for the convenience of people, but also for the sales people to spot the shoplifters easily. That's why your counter is by the door, to nab them as they walk out with something."

I remember when the first orders came in and boxes were all over the place. Al explained each step. First the counting, pricing, coding, and sizing on the tags. It took days. Tagging samples was the most confusing; all were different.

Adjusting Together

A good beginning each day set my body clock best—I was not a morning person.

Before opening the store, Kent usually went upstairs for his necessary coffee. He unlocked the gate for me since I drove fifteen miles to work and might be late. He put the cash in the register, turned on the lights and stereo, and got change from the bank upstairs if necessary. I noticed how fast my dark-haired assistant manager worked. When boxes came in, he quickly slit, sorted, and counted. I was slower, but wanted to be sure the order was complete.

I thought he drove himself too much, though he was pleasant and very capable at selling menswear to our customers. Much better than I was, he knew all the tricks some characters used to pilfer. As the store was being new and not very busy, I figured he must be restless and bored at times. I guess he got a charge out of our new computerized cash register, plunking keys all the time he was near it, even when we had no sales. It was a complicated one for me with many functions, if you know how to use it well.

I couldn't always explain to Charles what some figures meant on the tape, or why it didn't balance. He was not happy then, to say the least. Did the plunking do it? I didn't know. But Kent and Tanya became good friends, which was nice because he lived alone.

Brown-haired Tanya, a soft-spoken, proud mother of two pretty girls who often came with her husband to the mall, liked my store very much. She said, "I'd prayed for this job and enjoy the work." Her experience and friendly personality helped and she arranged displays well also. She quickly chose and bought for her girls pretty things in stock, which was good advertising, as they told their friends. When she called in sick, for herself or her girls' care, I changed her plans to work on her day off, or called my girls Lisa and Kim to work, which they liked. I liked to have them around.

Lisa, my alterations gal, besides being capable at selling, was my buying expert. She had experience in bigger cities, so I consulted her often each week. *Very impressive,* I thought. Did I feel inferior? Not really, knowing I was top dog down there. I learned that this also had drawbacks.

This was a family affair. Kim lived about thirty miles away and had three little ones. She only worked now and then. At Christmas time, I would need all. While in college, she was a salesgirl in a big store upstairs. Both girls had more experience than I, but I learned. For example, I didn't want to sell jeans in my store. I thought they weren't any fun to sell and were expensive to stock. The help insisted I must–it would be a basic item, and as it turned out they were right. Jeans did fill much shelf space, and with kids so particular about labels, I didn't want to compete with those upstairs stores–forty dollars–plus for jeans? Because of the brand name? That was asinine, if you asked me, but no one did. I stocked the brands with lesser known names, cute ones that really sold.

Then there were our neighbors. Gwen, from the gift shop next door, was a nice, chatty gal who offered many tips. She displayed wicker, oriental, and exquisite pieces, sold joke gifts, pottery, candles, incense, and wall hangings. She hated it when the kids tried to scare the tarantula and poke at the tiny crabs. She dropped by a couple of times a day or we visited in the hall.

The shop across from us, for the full-figured and moms-to-be, was the only one of its kind in town. Some of those customers were nicely plump, some were short and squat and waddled. But then others were really tall and wore their weight well, looking sharp with new items they bought from the owner, Sue. But because the long stairway was a killer for her average clientele, Sue was not happy down there and wanted to move upstairs. Many people didn't know her shop existed downstairs.

She and I discussed a plan, with sketches, to make our hall a mini Bourbon Street, each shop having a store lamp and quaint decor to match. A sign upstairs would repeat the theme name and entice people downstairs. The beauty shop down the hall was a very busy place and that could make it a jumping little street. There was a mini colored fountain down the hall, like a wishing well. Little ones watched it like they did the big one upstairs in the hall.

My scarecrows, especially John in my show window, caught the eyes of the people coming from the elevator behind the stairs, or as they wandered down and looked over the railing. My sign beside the door frame was an eye-catcher, drawn by our youngest girl, Lea: a scarecrow sitting in an antique car, with packages in the rumble seat. I liked the idea the more I thought of it. We were rolling along, weren't we?

Training the Help

Then my bubble burst.

One day Al meandered in. He had not done that before, likely because he wasn't paid to. He roamed all over the store. I remembered the salesmanship lecture he gave to the sales people before the store opened. I worried, as he reminded me of a few points I forgot and store policies he made that I neglected a bit, like:

- Do you know all about your products, sizes, fabrics, styles, and prices compared to your competition?
- Do you make excuses when your alterations aren't back when promised or new items expected are not yet in?
- I hope you don't say, "May I help you?" You should say, "It's nice to see you," or "What can I show you?" Tell them, "You made a good choice, you'll like it."
- Do you watch their body language, like touching a nose means they're in doubt, or shifting their body means they're restless and don't like the item?
- Feeling the object shows interest as does reading the label. If they have to "ask spouse" or "will come back later," say, "It could be gone."
- Offer layaways but no refund. Eye contact shows sincerity. If he nods agreement, but doesn't want it rung up, ask questions. Why delay? Price not right? Quality not suitable? Try it on?
- Do you have sales meetings with your help to review ads? Do you encourage them? Or have them keep a want list? An out of stock list? Do you call the names of those whose ordered items arrived?

I knew I looked frustrated, even a bit angry. He really laid it on me about letting people out the door so easily. I thought he was "hard sell," and I wasn't. He said, "The store looks drab and should be rearranged with racks closer."

Really? Well, I knew we had to watch the customers, so we could not have them too close, and said so. But he didn't agree. He claimed, "Your price tags don't show a big enough discount since this is a discount store."

When I told Charles that night about Al's visit, I decided that Al never worked with clothes, so I couldn't follow all his advice.

"Sometimes you have to follow your own common sense, or what you like for your customers, you know," Charles advised.

"Al did admit he shouldn't come in because he tends to be too critical. He sure was!" I muttered.

The sales help wasn't too impressed at the time of the lecture. All were experienced in selling clothes and other kinds of goods, and thought much of the lecture did not apply to us. "But some of it was a good reminder, and we tried to start right," they admitted. "That's retail for you."

I swallowed my pride, remembering, For a manager, the buck stops here!

Advertising

Do consumers hear and read ads, really? Seriously? Often? I thought, My store must be important, why else does that nice lady from the radio station come in so often? I knew one of our new plants decorating the counter was sent from her station when we opened, but I didn't ask her to come back. I soon realized the way advertising works.

All the radio stations had heard we were there, and sent their reps every week to sign us up for some radio spots. I told Tanya, "I'm getting weary of all the requests to advertise. I tell them Charles makes the decisions, so they explain their ad plans and come back to hear what he wants. There are five stations; newspapers check every week, too."

Tanya asked, "Does it cost much to have ads? I have seen the samples you post behind the counter and they don't look big at all. I heard ours on the radio last week, I changed stations to listen, remember?"

I did–then it was back to our country western music.

"It sure does cost. It takes a big bite of my profits to sign those radio and newspaper contracts for this year. I'm not making enough yet to afford it, but I'm told I can't afford not to, either. People don't know I'm here unless I tell and show them. Sue's business across the hall uses only billboards," I continued, "and those are switched around town every month. A rep tried to sell us that method, too, but we can't afford it. The suburban papers left samples and shopping news types want ads. That's how they make their money, but it does get tiresome. That's also how retail competes–the bigger the ad, the more people see it."

At times Tanya told the reps for me that we were not interested or gave their business cards to me to call them back. It's a dog-eat-dog business, whatever that means.

There was another kind of promotion, too–the coupon flyers. People cut out those little squares that give some cents or dollars off certain items in the store, or a rate off their whole bill. We hadn't tried that, but I planned at Christmas to send a sales flyer to people on my mailing list and give a coupon. I had about five hundred names by then that would reward my special customers who liked my bargains. Flyers cost a bundle in postage and printing, plus the time to address and fold them. Nothing was easy in retail, I found, slowly but surely.

"Lifted"

I learned the hard way, that's an abbreviation with a four-letter word in front, when spelled correctly.

No one came from the elevator or down the steps for a long time that evening. It was dead in the hall, so I rested my feet during the quiet dinner hour. Ah, there was someone! A tall, black, curly-haired teenager. He looked past John the scarecrow and the sparkling silver Christmas tree in the store window into the store and at me. I liked to watch the shoppers walk by our open door, but their entering was the desire of my heart, of course. Well, he came in, heading toward scarecrow Cecil's area and looking at all the jacket racks. He was wearing a thin, tan windbreaker and a gray knit hat. After trying on enough jackets to wear them and me out, he didn't make up his mind, and left the store.

I noticed he came and went another time, seeing himself in the mirror on the store support pillar. I had tried to help him choose between puffy polyester or down outer coats. One blue coat with red and light blue trim he called a girl's style, and rejected it fast. He said, "Have to talk to my mom upstairs," as he left.

I watched the area while eating in the back room doorway, because no one else was there, but I became uneasy and checked the racks. Then he came the third time to look at the jackets. "I'm back from my mother," he mumbled, "checking with her before deciding." I wished he would make up his mind; so far he had spent about twenty minutes of my time as I showed all jackets in his size. Other customers came into the store about that time, so I was busy.

A man and lady wanted to see sweaters and blazers; a family group browsed while the man sat on the bench in the children's play area. After

I wrote the woman's purchase on a credit card holder and bagged her sweater and blazer, I looked around the store. Where was everybody? That coat customer? Finally gone? When did he leave? I never noticed, but then wondered. Something bothered me.

I examined the jacket rack of salesmen's samples; there hung a very lonely black hanger, with no blue and red jacket on it, like the one hanging next to it. I looked both ways out the window, also out the door, feeling helpless and cheated. The husband of a beauty shop employee began to climb the stairs, so I asked him to wander down the mall and watch for a black-haired boy wearing or carrying a blue jacket like the one in my hand. My first shoplifter! He agreed to. Because I had spent so much time with the kid, I was angry, too. When the man returned he said, "No luck. He probably went to his car right away."

Being ripped off is humiliating. I thought the boy was shy, didn't speak up, and I wanted to be helpful. The next day I briefed Kent and Tanya about the incident and what the boy looked like. I really didn't expect him to return, since he'd be identified, but he did. Charles and I were gone for a weekend. No one working knew it was him for sure; Kim and Lisa could have been ripped off badly. He took a ski sweater, slipping it under his tan jacket. He still wore that hat. He found my store a "soft touch" and probably invited his friends. I didn't know what to do. I couldn't afford enough help to fight that at Christmas time! Kent was trained for it, but wouldn't work at night because of his other job.

I heard that the next time "sticky fingers" entered wearing my jacket with a girlfriend and two friends. Tanya recognized him and worried. She stood near his friends in one corner; his girlfriend moved to another corner. Then Tanya called Kent for help at the counter, but warned him. As he used the telephone to call the police, the hood glared at him. My flashy blue jacket dashed down the hall to the back door. The others wanted to follow him but were not sure which way to go. So much for that day. Good ol' Kent!

The next time I saw my jacket again, the thief waved at me while I was on my counter phone by the door. He entered the gift/drug paraphernalia shop across the hall. What gall!

I hoped he knew we all had him pegged by then, but that did not make my day. Shoplifting became a way of life for me, the "laid back grand-mother/owner."

Tricked

Later Kent told me that on another day while my store was really busy–which I liked–the men's department had a suspicious-looking character in the fitting room. Kent was alone, but he had his eyes peeled. At the door as the man tried to leave, Kent called him, "Come back and take off our pants." He cleverly tried to sneak out with them under his own.

But he returned to the fitting room with another pair, one he slipped from the shelf. Kent waited for him. He covered up the pair he lifted under the new pair in his hands to make it look like he did not have any others. Kent ordered, "Do not enter this store again!"

Then the man asked Kent, "Haven't I seen you somewhere before?"

"Yes, I'm the security man at another store in town." The shoplifter answered, "Okay, I won't be back!" and dashed for the back steps.

We all took turns working alone in the store, but with those scarecrows around, I seemed to be in relaxed company. I could imagine it anyway, and I muttered to them under my breath when frustrated with problems. I kept myself under control, an image I decided I should maintain. The scarecrows didn't model new clothes, they only held them. I heard someone suggest my store should have mannequins but I said my "crows" gave it proper class.

Firing, Hiring, or Not To

We had a great holiday/first year-end sales, so the extra salesgirl I hired worked out fine. We gave all the sales help a bonus and looked for a happy new year. But a new problem surfaced. With holiday shopping over, business would slow down, people said. What about Kent? Tanya? We needed only part-time help, and Kent did have another job. A man for the men's department wasn't necessary after all, since more women shopped for the men than men did themselves. I wondered about that, and watched to see how consistently that happened. Men often took their wives in to help them make decisions, I noticed.

I have told Tanya, "With refunds and exchanges given at first, that rush is likely over. I'm rather glad the holiday is over. Knowing our greatest sales come from a religious holiday doesn't help–it makes or breaks us. That's retail.

Charles, the financial advisor, made the decision one evening at home. Next day, I sadly stared out the door, mulling over the situation. When he called Kent to the back room I couldn't hear what he said, but I knew, and wasn't interested. I worked with the young man; we became friends and it wasn't easy to face this business alone.

Suddenly Kent came out with his coat, looking very serious. He walked fast out the door, with a quick "bye" to me. I felt his humiliation at being fired so soon from his assistant manager position. I didn't know if it was a normal procedure to praise a person you worked with, but I sent him a letter and also wished him well in the future.

In my business generally, I couldn't believe the number of people who applied for a job. Some were so persuasive; many of the girls were cute, too. Even a handsome college student who was not going back to school wished a job as he was out of funds. I had lots of applications on file.

There was a winner who had been in many times, a man who looked very intense, with dark beard and clothes and piercing eyes. He wanted to work as a mime in the hall, to attract the kids and their moms. He was the most desperate, poor guy. He would do bookkeeping, fixing, cleaning, anything. He even wanted me to "job train," he said. I could collect funds from the state to teach him retail and pay him a bit, also.

I told Tanya, "I'd like to give them work to do; I feel so sorry for them when they walk away." Often only my signature on their unemployment form was wanted to collect their compensation, but most would like to work. The recession, or slump as some customers called it, was really sad.

With Kent gone, I had to mail, unpack, and shove the boxes myself, though Charles handled the heavy stuff up and down the stairs or freight elevator. That was a heavy beast to maneuver, with the access door across the hall. I had to wait indefinitely, if someone left the elevator upstairs or disconnected somewhere. We were allowed an area for storage that was not pleasant–broken windows, locks, piles of junk not removed by the previous owner, and inadequate lights. But then, no one charged us. We picked a small room and added a new lock to the door. I knew first hand now: Life was no bed of roses.

Mobbed

When the cat's away, anything can happen to the mice!

One Saturday Charles and I traveled to Tennessee on a buying trip. Later we were told that only a few customers had been in; Tanya was alone for awhile and heard an awful racket. Suddenly a flock of teenagers came in, nine maybe. She could not watch them all, as they spread around the store at once. She answered questions on all sides. They were casing the place. She became nervous and afraid, they were so noisy and rude. Her husband was due back soon from shopping upstairs.

She called for Sue across the hall since she was unable to reach the counter to phone with all the commotion. When her husband returned, the kids left out the back hall door but he followed them, to her great relief. He described what happened. The police in the alley did catch a couple of kids with stuff on them from upstairs stores–it must have been wild. They had to drive out a mob of 200 kids running through the mall, bumping shoppers and yelling.

Later I discovered one of the samples I liked, a green crepe de chine two-piece dress, was missing. It had hung on Elsie's left arm and likely was stolen the day the mob rushed in. That was so disappointing to me, when shoplifters took my especially pretty items. I remembered, "That's retail."

Fighting City Hall

What a boring morning! No kids pulled Elsie's straw hair or punched her overhanging belly. No boys looked at any nylon vests. And women's "after five" coordinates didn't get a glance from the matrons. It was enough to make me weep: only a couple of browsers and a sale of thermal underwear.

I was working at the counter preparing for my next buying trip when a man approached me, not buying, obviously. He didn't look around to see my layout, but pulled out his wallet. He flashed a card before my eyes and said, "I want to show you my identification first." His voice was serious. Some kind of inspector, I guessed. "Did you put up that flashing sign by the elevator upstairs?" So that was it, more hassle on that thing.

I explained, "No, merchants in the lower mall here did."

"Who put that sign up?" he repeated.

"The building owners allowed us to have it installed. They checked it out before it was done and said the one-foot extension beyond the elevator was permitted," I informed him.

He was about my height, and we looked at each other eyeball to eyeball while he insisted, "Who put that sign up?

"Rotar Sign Company, with management approval," I said.

He growled, "Well, it's illegal and has to come down."

I didn't flinch. "You'll have to tell the management."

Out went the city inspector as fast as he came. He said to the cop who came down with him, "Rotar Sign put it up." Funny what some power does.

Three of we business gals downstairs waited three months for the installation of that simple sign, which merely read, "Lower Level," for people to know there was a downstairs mini-mall. Between the landlords stalling and bad weather delays, we were lucky to get it up before February. Sidewalk sales were just over upstairs! So typical. When a city commissioner friend passed by later, I told her. She could not understand why businesses must take that, and wondered what provoked that complaint. She promised to find out why no alternatives were given to me.

That powerful inspector finished his job. I was called by Rotar Signs. "The sign must come down or else." But the sales rep planned to negotiate a solution and would drop by afterwards to tell me, which he did. He wasn't as sad as I expected he would be. I knew him, as he'd been in before about signs, our logo, painting, repainting, colors, and designs.

Evidently Mr. Inspector was discourteous to the Rotar man, too, which figured.

"You owe money for a permit to put up the sign," the Rotar man stated, "but he charged you twice as much as is required, just to be difficult. I told him he was only hurting the merchants; our company's paid and repeated it when the turkey threatened to remove your sign to smash it."

It appears his city manager saw the sign and got on his back, which got the pot boiling. It was to be moved a little to the left and the *flashing* removed, though the light could stay on. That was the only place in the city it was required. Mr. Big reduced the permit properly also, thanks to the Rotar man, and I paid the fee.

But that news traveled! Cissy, my petite neighbor from the beauty shop came in, angry because our flashing had to be removed. She had heard that one of the owners threatened to sue the city if they took that sign down. Well, peace reigned again after all was explained, accepted, and the dust settled. Boredom was no longer in my store vocabulary, and city hall was an ogre.

Baby-sitting

What's a family business? Merely a ma and pa affair? There were times when the downstairs commotion in my area was my fault, to a degree. When my little people and grandchildren dashed out of the elevator, the plaything for most kids downstairs, many things happened.

Elsie's belt was loosened by them, and her straw belly almost fell to her knees. They were playful busy bodies, and Kim's little boy liked to flit between racks, whip off price tags hanging from the garments, or race up and down the stairs and hall. Cute, but watch out. His chubby sister might color pictures on the spool table or parade around with an open umbrella, bumping racks. She locked one of the long fitting-room doors from the inside, but was sent under to unlock it again by her mom.

The oldest one, Lori, helped dress, stuff, and tie the crows. She named John, in the window, dressed in her daddy's clothes. When the boy escaped upstairs, his mother didn't miss him because she was trying on some jeans and sweaters. I flew out to catch him before he disappeared–that's what grandmas do, business or no business. But my show window was the prime challenge.

Many little ones wanted to climb the rail fence to play in it. The cedar chest had a great cover to slam shut noisily, and the cowbell really rang an ear off you. When hit, the milkweed pods in the basket shed fluffy seeds that just hung in the atmosphere, waiting to be caught or bloom. My guitar, leaning on crow John, could have been sold ten times, though one string was missing. My rooster clock hanging above the chest enticed little boys to move the hands.

But an old black milk can that rattled frustrated children as the cover would not come off. My gold tea kettle was an antique; not real gold, just painted. I wondered what made the spider plant the radio station gave me stay alive, as no daylight reached down there, but I didn't appreciate it spilling dirt when tipped by little feet. Though I tried to have all items only for looks, I seldom won. My chubby girl plucked the eyes off Stuffy Tiger hugging him by the neck, or hugging Eager Beaver by his tail, which came loose.

Their dad entered and everything was under control again. Tim liked my "duds," as he called them: shirts, velours, a jacket, and some of our jeans, too. So they bought, what could I say? But all relaxed when Kim's family left for the ice-cream store upstairs.

Now Lisa's little boy, in the creeping stage, would hide under the clothes racks and wagons. She left him with me to dash upstairs a couple of times, but he'd bellow for her if she were gone long, which was not conducive to running a peaceful store. It was a family business, all right!

Being Friends

I found a new friend, Rose, accidentally, and we were attracted to each other over night. We both had time on our hands and many of the same interests, reading and writing for instance. Rose loved to come from her mother's store just outside the mall where she worked, too. She acquired handicaps from an accident when she was a teenager: impaired vision and facial scars. We just loved to chat.

It seemed the height of the ridiculous, what we could find to talk about. I suppose we sounded like we enjoyed bad memories. But then, nothing's ever right in life, and Rose felt a little divine improvement would be welcome, so we talked about God. She was a very religious Catholic and attended mass every noon, often stopping in on the way back. I, a Protestant, enjoyed it, finding a great many common opinions and inspirations. I invited her to my writer's group a couple of times, trying to revive Rose's interest in an old hobby of her school days, something creative.

Rose also wanted male friendship but thought anyone would get a whiff of her condition if he hung around long enough, then take off. Poor thing. Our tête-à-tête resulted in both of us feeling better.

It was tragic for her to be so injured by a drunken driver. She bought a pretty blue raincoat from my stock, looking perky with her dark hair. She tried on sweaters, shirts, and skirts, too, just for fun. Life was quite routine for her so my shop in the mall broke it up a bit. I met her mother in her shop during a lunch break, and loved the sewing crafts, supplies, and finished pieces she displayed. She had heard about me, of course, so this good feeling was mutual.

Losing Neighbors and Coping

One morning, I noticed a man passing my show window carrying boxes to the elevator, and I recognized him finally. He was the owner of the gift shop next door, who worked occasionally when his sister, Gwen, or his wife couldn't. I remembered the previous month he said, "If my shop doesn't make enough at Christmas time, I will move to the second floor." I surmised he didn't make enough.

I realized that was bad for the other businesses in our hall, as his oddities like crabs, tarantula, and curios that drew children also drew adults to see the rest of us. The tarantula had died, though I didn't mind much. I would miss my chat with Gwen while she smoked by the hall ash receiver, as she was not allowed to smoke inside the store. It gave odor to the wicker? Well, I figured on our breaks we could go up or downstairs to talk if it was important, until I remembered we both worked alone most of the time, meaning we couldn't leave our stores. Yes, I would miss her.

Eventually, I saw their new shop. It was smaller, but much lighter, and on the second floor where more people went by. The royal blue carpet really accented the delicate, lovely pieces they had. I liked it. But my black hole next door was too quiet, like a huge tomb and deadening for us, I thought. I worried a bit; less traffic flow past my door netted lousy sales, so doom and gloom.

One afternoon, a strange woman rushed in with no coat on. She came by elevator and approached me with news. (She was employed at a store upstairs.) She warned, "Your store-room on the third floor is flooding and boxes are getting wet!" My boots and extra down jackets, the other half of our first shipment! I asked Tanya to mind the store while I hurried up to look. I hoped the jackets could be cleaned.

Down, or goose feathers, made a very soft, warm, but expensive jacket; the most valuable goods we sold. I wondered what caused the flood, as there were no rest rooms up there, I thought. I found out soon enough and rushed to the phone to call Charles. "A pipe froze up there because of a broken window, then burst. Water covered the floor of our storage room and the one next door. Come over after work to get the boxes off the floor, and help me take wet jackets out to be cleaned. Boots are in soaked boxes, too." Then I added, "And I hate to be in that dark hall alone this time of day. The alley bums sleep there when it's cold outside and might be there now for the night." What a pain!

So I said a prayer and walked up the two flights with my flashlight, as the second floor had no daylight and broken glass, plaster, and wood littered it. Because our door lock was broken by the man who searched for the water source to his storage room next door, I had told Tanya, "People could steal the coats easily and I want to shut the door, or make it look locked till Charles gets here. If I don't return soon, have someone come to check what happened to me. Such troubles!"

I knew those jackets could smell musty if wet too long, but wondered how long it had been. A day or two, maybe? They were washable, but could shrink; then they would not be considered new. It seemed funny to me that washed jeans were in, not jackets. That evening we moved everything to another room and installed a new lock. I had heard the phrase, "I can cope," and now believed it anew.

Defining and Measuring

People–yes, people! Sometimes when I wasn't busy, I noticed the different kinds of people who came through the store in a day. These were my analytical observations:

First, there are browsers, who flit through a store, glance at each counter, rack, or wagon, casing the place. Thirty seconds.

Second, the handlers, who feel the goods, note prices to compare upstairs, and linger undecided. Three minutes.

Third, there are "like items," who try on many, parade before mirrors, but will think about it. Ten minutes.

Fourth, I liked the shopper determined (usually men) on an item wanted; they ask, price it, take it. Two minutes.

Fifth, those noncommittal, just looking, have no money people. Five minutes.

Sixth, or those who "just discovered the store," who like the goods and prices, buy two of a kind, and will be back. Five minutes.

Seventh, had a few refunders, for any reason: button broke, don't like it, doesn't fit, wrong color, neck too tight (can't get it over child's head, but thirty year-old adult can), bought two, but only needs one so wants money back; or changed my mind.

The layaways, or holds, for lack of money now; might be sold; in a hurry, need a try-on, but not now.

All this made life interesting around there. People pulled surprises all the time and with a straight face. I wondered if my naiveté, amateur condition caused many of my problems in retail.

For instance, a new experience with more significance than meets the eye: I noticed a man who tried on a pair of dress pants. He said he had seen a special earlier and wondered if the price had been reduced. When I told him not yet, he asked, "Would you reduce it if I bought it now?"

So I asked, "Which pair? Could knock off altering cost to hem it."

He went to the rack of pants and took one. "This blue check would go great with a shirt I have, but I can't afford it otherwise. I could put it on layaway and get it on my next paycheck." I offered a deal.

"Well, try it on and I could let it go for two dollars less, since it's past the winter season." While he wore it at the big mirror near crow Cecil, I measured and pinned up the hem for him. He really fidgeted. I chatted, as we were alone in the store, but fitting a man's pants wasn't my forte, obviously. Then he commented. "Lower in the back, for a pair of boots I have."

"Do you know your inseam?" I asked.

"No." But that I did not pursue. Noticing his nervousness and snug fit, I pinned the front quickly. Luckily a girl came in for a quick sale from the wagon, so I took it, and the youngish man went back to the fitting room to change. That had been Kent's job before.

Next he handed the pants to me at the counter, gave his name and phone number for Lisa to call when ready and left, thanking me. I muttered to myself, "I don't want to do that again, nor does he, I'm sure."

That's retail for you, facetious, among other things.

Meeting the Landlord

To miss this unbelievable, ridiculous event would be sad, I decided.

One noon, just after I ate my yogurt, crackers, and fruit, I walked to the counter, pulled out a new salesmen's catalog, and made notes of likely goods to order. With no customers around, I knew it was the best time. Call it dead time? Not even little kids in to color, or women to try on boots, or bored husbands resting on benches.

Suddenly the music from my stereo speakers was interrupted by a forceful man marching through the wide doorway and greeting me with, "I want to talk to the owner of the store. Is he here?" He wore glasses and a dark suit, and had a balding head.

"I'm his wife," I said pleasantly.

He informed me, "I'm one of the landlords, Mr. Trunkle. I checked with Mr. Murch and found that no rent has been paid since your store opened eight months ago. You owe thousands and here's our notice of it." He handed me a pink legal sheet with figures; his signature and some words caught my eye.

"That can't be," I denied emphatically. "We've paid our rent every month, and I can get the check numbers for you. I do not understand, we've sent them to Mr. Murch's office as often as the lease stipulated."

He looked surprised. "January and February, too?"

I glared at him, "Of course!" I had heard about this man from our neighbors.

Then he asked, "You park in the lot behind the store, don't you?"

I answered, "Yes."

He gloated, "Well, you've never paid for that, have you?" What a character!

I declared, "No, no one ever specified any amount or details regarding parking, so we haven't." I wondered if these landlords knew what the other was doing, or even communicated.

Then he bellowed, "Well, you owe $30 a month for eight months for using that lot." He started to leave. "I'll check out that rent again. You paid it?"

"Yes, I'll get the check numbers for you," I retorted.

"No," he insisted, "I'll check it out; you pay for the parking!" And he left, speaking loudly as he went toward the hall. Thankfully no customers were in the store to hear him accuse me of such a dumb thing-and filling a store with family clothes. Sounded like the right hand didn't know what the left hand was doing. Oh, I couldn't wait to call Charles. So ridiculous!

Later Charles wrote Mr. Trunkle a scathing letter about publicly accusing his wife of a large debt–a falsehood, at that. Such was the nature of our landlord that my neighbors predicted we would definitely have to go to court, as they had to do sometimes. But wonder of wonders, ours was resolved quietly.

I sometimes wished others, besides my scarecrows, could witness the foibles of powerful people, and laugh with me. I learned in kindergarten to say I'm sorry when I hurt somebody. Guess he missed that lesson in philosophy on how to be.

Rearranging and Changing

Sue, my neighbor, had just rushed over to my counter where I stood, and blurted out some awful news. She said, "I'm closing my business in a month and a half, if I can stay here that long. I'm not going to fight this economy anymore and it's only going to get worse. I lose so much, waiting for the turn around. I plan to sell Fond Fanny makeup."

I asked, shocked, "You mean it? Just like that? It's going to be better here this spring."

"No, I don't expect so," she admitted.

"Your husband is out of a job; why not sell it outright, as you have a good thing, being the only maternity shop in town," I suggested.

"No, a store upstairs tried for a year to sell and it's worse, so I can't wait. The crummy landlords won't either. I have no lease."

I knew that left only three businesses downstairs; what a rotten development. It wasn't funny. Times were changing!

The upshot of Sue's closing, after a period of busy liquidation, was that I displayed and sold the leftover plus sizes from her store across the hall. To do this, the men's department was moved back and crows Cecil and Elsie were arranged closer to the door, holding more items temporarily.

I thought, Too bad they couldn't guard the bras and girdles rack for me, small items! Tanya complained someone took a bra; it was slipped from a box to a purse or pocket, or the girl tried it on and kept it; no one knew. Also I decided to shut the chain door two feet since I suspected someone slipped a skirt from the rack by the door that day. It was the size I had just put out; a brown border print was missing. Gwen, now working upstairs, had warned me that I should remove that rack from the door area at night. People used canes to unhook the hangers with items and grab them through the door openings.

What next! It was sickening; I had to be suspicious of people all the time to protect my clothes properly! Likely I could blame it on our changing neighborhood. I knew what was going on outside my shop. The loafers meandered by and whipped old cigarette butts from the ash receiver. Or the guy who picked up the empty pop cans for the change at the pop machine was about as well-dressed as my crows, poor soul. At times I watched a weirdo who picked up the candy in the ash tray and trash basket by the steps. Then it dawned on me what he was doing, since he stayed by the steps when he ate it. His dirty knit cap pulled down over his ears and forehead; he had a little beard. Never looked at anybody, just the floor and those containers. What a way to go!

I knew more about drug paraphernalia then before; I could see it on the counters across the hall. The tall red pipes attracted everyone's attention; the little stuff was near the back of the store, no doubt hidden by displays of hats, feathers, belts, jewelry, and frames. I was painfully aware it remained the only retail shop downstairs beside mine, and some of its customers looked like they crawled right out of the woodwork, not referring to their clothes but their spacey faces, dirty hair, and stooped walk. Maybe those characters kept some people away from my store?

Then I heard that the women's shop at the top of the stairs was closing. A big sign in the window read, WE HAD IT! The main floor wasn't utopia either; a slump was a bummer for everyone.

Trying "New Wrinkles"

There was a man who stopped by my window later, holding a blue file folder. When he left some books and a catalog for me to show Charles, he tried to persuade me to use a barter system with some other businesses. He said, "They trade services and goods: windows cleaned, car tires rotated, trees cut down, cars washed, sell sewing machines, carpets, and many other things. It allows those merchants to buy your clothes for units, which equal about one dollar per unit."

"I like the idea, and also the free advertising in the catalog, with your 150 members," I agreed. "And each month I would receive a new list so I'd know what goods and services?"

He'd been in other times when I wasn't or was busy. "Is that a new wrinkle? Only two or three other clothing stores on the exchange? All out of town?" I questioned.

"Yes, and this can be used all over the country with other exchanges, even for travel, for a 10 percent fee. No others in the mall are signed, so I would like you to be the first to join."

There was a lot to running a business. I wanted the billboard advertising method, and told Charles if he consented to be on the exchange, I could utilize the company that offered it. Our scarecrow logo would be the one on the billboard. My crows would have their smiling faces plastered all over town. I liked that idea. We never considered TV ads, and felt a business must be rich to do so. We spent hundreds of dollars for thirty-second spots and one-page shopping ads. Oh, no!

Then entered something to change my negative mood: a sharp dude wearing purple pants and a silk shirt. He knocked my eyes out. His silver jewelry and patent shoes really shone. He was handsome, too. But what a get-up! He probably turned the gals' heads upstairs. One thing about being in a clothing outlet-we drew all kinds to our bargains, but our styles were casual compared to that fashion plate. My beautiful salesmen's samples were fashionable, but people didn't pick them till they were marked way down. The crepe de chine, two-piece dresses were right from the big city, as were the after-five pants and skirts. I took home a hunter green silk suit because no one wanted such a fancy one. My pale yellow silk tie blouse was perfect with it. I wondered why so few customers wanted my quality and good brands at low prices.

Maybe the store name was not right? People told their friends where they bought it, I supposed. Retail for you? Tanya said so, "And the trouble with clothes is they're in style one season, out the next. So changeable! Peer pressure influences many, they wait for a sale. Then worry about being out of date." People are funny.

Dealing with Salesmen and Goods

How I loved new merchandise arrival! But that day the order was a big one. UPS brought in five boxes from the same company. Three more came from another man; he didn't use the elevator so I didn't see him at first. All men's jeans were due that week, I had told customers. They had been asking for more of the irregular basics and they moved fast. The cartons were heavy and I appreciated the driver delivering them into the store. They were not supposed to-union orders, I guessed. I remembered an order during the previous week. Another big one, with damaged kids' jeans and wet boxes falling apart. They were merely dropped off at the back door of the long hall and I had a rough time moving them onto the dolly. At least the women's robes were plastic wrapped, so not damaged, thankfully.

I used all the help I could get. I really liked it when some salesmen happened to find my store downstairs, after contacting customers upstairs. I acquired three new sources of overruns and close-outs in one week, including the children's lines. My men's sweat suits and women's spring line came from some southern companies I never heard of before-good and reasonable. Those men also looked over my racks advising me when I was low on items, and mentioned markdowns and good deals coming. I felt God smiling at me.

We were coming along nicely. When Mike Dida first came, Charles and I stopped at his motel room that night to see his lines and order. We were happy to not have to leave town to pick goods. He also attended the state shows every season and became my most understanding rep, calling about specials. I worried less about finding new styles in my price category, though I admitted I liked to buy the new items after the present season's were almost sold. Some stores used bank loans to tie them over, but that wasn't my way. It was how Mike stocked his daughter's store which was similar to mine. I told Lisa, "I can't afford many of one item like big stores."

"I know," replied Lisa. "I worried whether all I bought for Bixbe's big store would sell, and if not, I could be fired. You are small potatoes, so buy nothing too flashy or you'll be stuck with it," she advised, as we chose styles and prices.

One company with a good brand name pulled a fast one on me and allowed no returns. Of the three dozen corduroy jeans for men, I received mixed colors and sizes for only half of them; eighteen tan pairs came in one size, 36 XL for the rest. Lisa had to shorten them to various lengths. Also eleven of three dozen light green women's turtle necks came in one size–a problem! That's retail!

Adjusting Anew

Until I heard what was moving in next door from the manager himself, there was not much excitement after the other stores moved out. But no doubt we would have action around there with a game room penny arcade in two weeks, if they could get ready by then. That would bring people downstairs. The question was how to draw them into my store. Maybe it was sour apples, but what money is left after playing the arcade games? Well, wait and see. "Should break the monotony for us, anyway," I told Tanya.

Soon we noticed people walked by just to watch the progress of the remodeling. We heard them talk and the kids were excited. A store worker from upstairs predicted we'd have trouble with the boisterous kids and more shoplifters.

Tanya said, "Someone always thinks on the negative side, you know. I'm expecting the kids to buy more from us than before. It's possible; they have allowances and baby-sit."

"That pounding gives me a headache. How about you?" I asked Tanya.

"No, can't say that it does. I like the sound, the action."

"Are you afraid we will be ripped off more? I hear women predict a bad element is going to bother us," I asked.

"Don't believe everything you hear," she reassured me. "Rumors come with change, in this business especially."

She was right. We saw new people in our store. Mothers came with their little ones, or while the bigger ones played next door. And teenagers browsed, tried on items, and told their moms what we had for them; nothing wrong with that. But then I heard someone say that if the game room stayed open later than the rest of the mall, kids tended to break into the other businesses somehow. We were easy, right next door. I noticed police downstairs more, though, so I quit worrying. "Don't borrow trouble...it's free," I told myself.

Trusting or Not

"Tanya, did you see that little, sweet-faced, white-haired lady heading for the elevator?"

"No, I can't say I did," she answered my question.

"She was well-dressed, coordinated and all that, her hair freshly set. Her name is Katie. Let me tell you what happened. She stopped to check our tops, tried on some salesmen's samples, and bought one. But she worried all the time about her daughter's opinion, who usually buys her clothes for her. Katie takes a bus downtown for something to do when the weather is good."

Tanya turned briefly to answer a question from a customer, then back to me.

"Well, she asked me, if it isn't right, can I return it? A seven dollar blouse? But I agreed and we chatted till her bus was to come. Katie had mentioned her experience at Cissy's hair salon. She didn't like the way her hair looked two days after a set and called for her money back, but Cissy refused."

"Imagine that, after sleeping on it? I don't blame her," Tanya stated.

"I'm not joking. She ate lunch upstairs once and the pie was spoiled. She told the manager she wanted her money back, but he wouldn't give it." I felt sorry for that little troubled lady, but began to wonder if she imagined all that.

Well the next day, sweet Katie gave us a run for our money. She came back with the top. Said her daughter thought she had a similar one. Could she have her money back? Why, of course, my promise was a promise. She wanted nothing in exchange, as I had asked her to do.

Finally, I wondered whether I should be cool and remote, or warm and spontaneous as I'd like to be. Syrupy Katie, who stopped about every other week, bought something again: A skirt. She needed reassuring often that it looked great, as she wanted her daughter to like it. She paid for it and left, happy with our blooming friendship. She suggested I go to lunch with her sometime when my help was in. What could I say? I was impressed? Not really.

I began to learn more tricks to the trade fast. The next day Katie created a problem. It sounded like I didn't give her correct change that day before–about seven dollars off-and her daughter sent her to collect it. When I asked her for the sales slip, she didn't have it. That slip gave the whole trans-action: cost, tax, money taken and returned. I told her I would ask my accoun-tant (Charles) if he tallied yesterday's sales, and see if that amount was over. She must call me tomorrow. Katie left very disappointed because her instruc-tions were to come home with the money! She said in parting, "I can't come here to shop if I don't get it, you know."

I told Tanya, "So much for our friendship and the store's reputation. She doesn't think I'll give it back if I could."

Tanya was curious to hear about Katie again. I telephoned Katie's home. I supposed the daughter answered, as Katie was out. I informed her, "We have no amount over and no way to prove an error without a sales slip. Your mother said she emptied her billfold for you and found no more money, but did she stop elsewhere to spend it?" I knew it was their word against mine, but who was to judge? The daughter insisted it was my error, naturally.

"I'm sorry we differ, but my accountant claimed there was no overage; he's professional," I said.

Tanya declared, "That's retail. Did she say her mother will never come back again?"

"Oh, sure! I know how it feels to be blacklisted now."

Using Style Shows

To be honest, there wasn't much we downstairs retailers could ever do for kicks. Some days, just watching people was for the birds. And speaking of birds, I wished people were more like them; contented, for one thing. I could imagine talking to my crows like this: "We're in such an exciting business. Interesting people, funny people, lovely people, crummy people, snooty people and especially picky ones, yes. But that's retail."

Then one day, in my lethargic condition, a salesman used a pitch to persuade me to be one of the eight stores in the mall to take part in a style show upstairs. "That's called promotion, and the prettiest form of advertising," he said. "Models walk gracefully in your clothes before the spectators to stimulate a desire to buy them. Shows are the way to draw many people."

I knew the mall sponsored all kinds of shows up there: car shows, antique shows, farm shows, cycle shows, bazaars, Christmas and Easter shows, and home shows. This one would show summer styles for men, women, and children. Tanya's girls would be our models. Well, that set a firecracker under us and it turned out to be fun for all on a Saturday.

Then one thing led to another. More excitement! I planned and packed all sorts of clothes in boxes, really having fun; sort of like being in the mail order business. Nobody had been in to buy or order, but I chose some combinations and outfits for a style show I was asked to put on in my town fifteen miles away. It was for a class offered by the county social services department for women who were in transition or in a tough spot-widowed, divorced, but wanting to find jobs and needing training. I would speak to them about body care, the total woman, or something like that and I hoped to sell some clothes. Advertising again. What to wear to work that's moderately priced, properly dressed people make their own atmosphere, in a way. I wanted to help them, they were so uncertain. I found it fun and sold some items to the staff also.

Now that I was on a roll, I turned down no requests. Another style show came up, one for senior citizens at the junior college. A model planned to come by to try on some merchandise. The women's club sent a model the previous week for a show–a friend of mine–but I didn't have the petite length or her larger-sized tops, so she couldn't be of use after all. Should I enlarge my stock a bit more, I wondered. Why don't men model much? Too self-conscious?

My model arrived. She seemed to be a pleasant-looking, white-haired grandma, though a little large for my clothes. I listened to her daughter with her.

"My mother only wears expensive, well-known labels and has an image to keep up. I shop with her to find them; her friends expect her to look nice all the time. I don't think we'll find anything here." (Do tell!)

Then Mother tried on a large-sized velour robe, since she was tall. She had a sweet dignity. The all-weather coat looked great on her, though she needed a colored scarf because beige was not her best shade. A blouse was pretty, too, but her daughter didn't like it. The mom was nicer and more cooperative than she. It was kind of her to consider my store, as a bargain store such as mine was beneath the average type of shopper. Or is it all in the mind?

As Charles said one night, "Sometimes I feel like the Statue of Liberty here. Give me your poor, oppressed, downtrodden, my door is open. Something like that." Well, I bought the best I could find, but I bet him she wouldn't buy them afterward, even at my discount to models. True enough!

But not so next time around! There came a pretty young model for the Junior Achievement style show. She had a ball finding outfits; more than the three she needed and she could not make up her mind. A prairie skirt and crochet top looked great. So did the chino pants and a plaid blouse with ruffles. Then a blazer and white pants with a knit T-top showed off her thin figure the best. She was a happy little model and planned to buy at least two of the sets afterward! Telling her friends about my store was advertising I liked.

Some days mostly girls came in and if you'd seen one, you'd seen them all. I noticed the few rugged, good-looking guys who passed my door and wished they would come in. But they didn't shop much. Only the restless, pilfering type had been in the last day or two. However, I couldn't forget those senior citizen mall walkers who looked in to check for lowered prices some mornings. They were pleasant characters but bought so little. That's retail...

Enjoying and Hiring Again

"It is a good day," I said to Tanya, "though I must view this lovely day chiefly from the skylight again." I was rather glum just because our cash register conked out. I wished I could fix it, but instead I called the company again for reprogramming over the phone from another city. The last time I was flustered when I couldn't open it to make change, but the man next door simply pushed a button from underneath.

Enter a chick so chic! So lovely, so slender, with her jet-black hair so stylish. She wasn't from around our town I figured, judging by her outfit. She wandered around the women's section, marveling at our dressier things; she had not seen such good prices since moving from New York. She was cool! I liked her crisp, crystal clear comments! She felt things with pleasure, making me very happy. Well, something had to drop through the slats; so few people in town liked my fancy clothes.

This lady bought a crepe skirt and blouse, and after looking over other salesmen's samples with good labels, she put on layaway a French blue knit, two-piece dress. Pleased to get it for thirty dollars, too. She was a beautiful lady with a gracious air! I wondered if she'd be back. I hoped so. If not, I would write a note to remind her, as I did to people with layaways if they were overdue.

Next arrived a new saleswoman I needed to man tables upstairs in the mall for our first sidewalk sale. This experienced older lady who had wanted a job earlier and filled out an application form chatted with me about her qualifications. Her name was Angela and she seemed so pleasant. She had more experience than any of us, even Lisa, but had been unemployed since her old employer's business moved. She lived near downtown and could walk to work-very helpful in winter, as everyone else drove a long way. All of us had car problems, too, so there was "nothing to beat the feet," as they say. I hoped we could keep her after sidewalk sales for back-to-school sales, as that was a busy time; the kids needed help, the jeans had to be watched, and such sales gave us a boost. Summer was dullsville.

Using Sidewalk Sales

Such a hustle and bustle as we began the sorting and markdowns of kids' clothes in earnest, since the sale was also to be a close-out of the whole section. So few people bought their things then–and we didn't have much either; it was ironic. But a new children's outlet store, yard sales, and the big discount stores were too much competition for me. The recession made it worse, too.

Though our sidewalk sale upstairs made more work and took extra help, we remembered no one came downstairs during the sale upstairs in previous years. I rented big tables to display our clothes for three days, with markdowns from every department, not just kids. The sales started the next day. We packed boxes from the back room to carry the items; we needed old stuff cleaned out. I loved it.

We arrived early, before the mall opened, to fill the tables, tuck away our money box, and stash supplies and a folding chair, if needed. We had a spot along the wall by the fountain so we only had to face frontward to watch for shoplifting. It was exciting. The girls had a ball taking turns upstairs and down! One covered as messenger or manned the spot at their breaks. It seemed the people who brought items down to try on bought more than usual. Liked the prices?

We had to stay open nights while the sale was on because the mall was open, resulting in a longer day for everyone, but more sales also. At the end of the day, I took the money box and some tags downstairs, happy that the manager of the closing ladies' store upstairs allowed our tables to remain there overnight. So kind of her, otherwise we'd have a hassle carrying everything down and up again each morning. Everyone sure looked tired as it was.

I guessed it was worth it, though; besides being pleased with each day's take, the whole thing gave us a wonderful ego massage. We were like the upstairs shops! And action was all around. People I knew stopped to talk, surprised that was my business, or not knowing I had one downstairs.

R & R and Parking

Rest and relaxation? What's that?

Little irritations with facilities were common, as when fitting room lights flickered, or overhead bulbs burned out. Sometimes I didn't care, as the men didn't use their change room often, and being in a dark corner the women didn't see the extra fitting room. Mirrors on pillars had needed more light, so were more important to me. It was a big nuisance for our sales family to use restrooms way down the hall and to fill our water pot for coffee and plants there. We had to shut and lock the big chain gate, a bother, then set down the pot to open the heavy gate, shoving the stubborn thing back. What a pain! Sometimes the neighbors watched our store for a couple of minutes, as we girls did for them when asked. Sadly, two stores moved away. We went through that rigamarole when we trudged to the bank for change, too.

The ultimate frustration one day was after an excited operator came from the hair salon. She told me a tow truck was hooking up my car in the parking lot behind the store to tow it away. I couldn't believe it! Leave the store just then? Out of the question. Angela went to the bank. I must pay if towed away, the operator said. I paid to park there! Besides, it was raining outside. I paced the floor, not knowing what to do. Why would my car be hauled off? Parked in the wrong spot?

Finally I asked the girl to mind the store while I checked, since Angela didn't return. Would Cissy object? "Always something to keep the pot a'boilin," I grumbled. Angela came back shortly after I left. No problem.

But as I angrily explained to Angela later, rushing back in with my hair all wet, "The upshot was I had to pay fifteen dollars to the tow truck operator. He had my car up and was ready to take off! I had parked behind some plumber's truck who had my spot, with my bumper a bit in the alley. The police were waiting and said I must pay, though the kids in the truck were illegally parked and called the tow man. When I asked them for money, they refused and wouldn't give their plumber boss's name either. They knew they were guilty. The policeman just drove away without asking the name for me. What a bummer!

"I want Charles to deduct it from next month's parking fee–let the landlord put up reserved signs to be fair to the tenants. But why would he start now?" I added. Relaxation? "No rest for the wicked," they say, "and the righteous don't need any."

Worrying or Not, and Resigning

After the back to school sales ended, I told Tanya, "I'm wondering what I'm buying wrong, if anything. When people don't come in for a couple of hours, I figure it's the merchandise, though the location is partly to blame. That prospect blows my mind, too. I flick through the racks, counting and complaining to myself!"

The jeans I unpacked that day had six pair of size 30-36. Now that's for a skinny, tall guy. And the rest of the order wasn't mixed at all. So I asked Lisa to shorten some. The assorted sweaters for men came in with bad flaws. Companies were dumping bunches on my little store which I couldn't return. I had no control of sizes; that worried me. I had to sell them to pay for them, usually in sixty days. I felt Charles should resolve the problem as he ordered them.

Tanya hoped it eased my doubts of my judgment to say, "That's retail for you."

Of course, no one cared but me, the boss, and I said, "I have a thick skin, give it to me straight." But she only laughed.

Adding to my concerns was the fact Tanya became sick occasionally and her husband discussed it with me one day. I heard him hint she might not want to work alone anymore, since the game room next door attracted some weirdoes. Of course, the headshop across the hall did, too, so I could say, "We're in a challenging spot, all right."

Shortly after, Tanya delivered her resignation while I was out to the bank; she was ordered to rest for some weeks and solve a few problems. I felt badly, for I would soon plan my Christmas schedule, though I couldn't risk many absences as everyone worked more, not less at that time. I would miss Tanya. She had said, "I will miss all of you and the store."

I could use Angela and Lisa more, no doubt, which both liked as they worked well together. So the season began with the three of us pulling our oars hard. The orders began to arrive, the Christmas tree again blinked in the show window and the chilly weather meant my down jackets might be bought again. We still had many boxes of them, and I supplemented those with new styles and sizes of polyester quilted and plain fabrics. I found a few women's winter coats of good brands and basic sizes and colors, so I felt prepared. Lovely mitten and scarf sets from a new source in Chicago filled the wagon by the counter.

That week I felt the first bit of Christmas spirit, as a slightly plump customer with a winning smile came in looking for Christmas presents to lay-away. She was a young mom with an unemployed husband who worked down the street and shopped on her lunch hours. She set many items aside, as she had some young ones, and would pay on her bill occasionally, she said. By her being so happy to find our store, giving her family Christmas after all, she made my day.

She bought a sweater for each family member, some pants, and hat and scarf sets, and would be back for more after she figured sizes of others. Her enthusiasm was catching. It made it all worthwhile after days of poor sales, or fuss budgets, or wrong sizes sent, and returns that cost time and money to UPS. We had an uplifting chat, too; I was glad for that just then. I noted everyone had their worries, and thought of my motto hanging on the back wall above my work table: Don't Be Afraid To Fail. Good advice. Under it this was printed:

"You've failed many times, although you may not remember. You fell down the first time you tried to walk. You almost drowned the first time you tried to swim, didn't you? Did you hit the ball the first time you swung a bat? Heavy hitters, the ones who hit the most home runs, also strike out a lot...R. H. Macy failed seven times before his store in New York caught on. English novelist John Creasey got 753 rejection slips before he published 564 books. Babe Ruth struck out 1,330 times, but he also hit 714 home runs. Don't worry about failure. Worry about the chances you miss when you don't even try." (Anonymous) My friend Rose liked it so well she had copies of it made for others.

Maintaining and Refunding

One night I noticed how bored Charles was. He hated to come in on Friday nights to keep me company because it had been so dead lately. He marched up and down the aisles, checked on Al's tips for something to do. He wouldn't wait on customers; he couldn't work the cash register. I asked him to watch for shoplifters. He carried stock and empty boxes to and from the storage room; he fixed the door's electric eye when it didn't work; usually kids bumped it so the beam missed. He replaced light bulbs that burned out each week until a nice young salesman ordered new ones for me that would last twelve months or more. Since wiring was loose in some fixtures, off went the power to prevent a shock. Some place!

I said, " I could use a servant at home, too. I've devoted my life to this business, and keep it clean, with Angela's help."

He said, "Fat chance." He vacuumed for me at home, though, and bought groceries when he thought of it. He even started dinner at times, so what could I say?

Suddenly, in bustled a serious shopper, one who knew what she wanted. She had dark hair, was tall, wore glasses, and was middle-aged. By the back fitting rooms, she whipped through the racks like a house a fire, looking at prices. She sounded a bit flaky to me, talking to herself, but then, I talk to myself, too. When she headed for the counter I couldn't keep up with her. As she left, she said, "I'll be back when my check comes in."

I told Charles, "She's all right. Menopause is probably knocking loudly at her door."

We remembered the busy shopper from that last Friday night–she came back, a week later. Retracing her steps to the women's racks, she scooped an armful–suits, pants, tops, and a raincoat; had the time of her life trying them on. If she bought half of those, we'd have the best sale of the week; Charles would jump for joy. She came to the front, oh, so happy, pulling out a wad of bills to pay for most of what she tried on. Her check had come in, all right! *She had a good memory*, I thought.

Well, not really, some bad news on Monday. A lady approached the counter to talk to me. She had the bags of clothes our best sale bought Friday night, with a sales slip. She and her husband wanted the money back. She informed me, "Our sister left town, took a bus south this weekend to live with a relative, and has asked us to return all those clothes she bought. Since she has no need of them in a warm climate, and they don't fit any relatives here, a refund would be best." Imagine that! She must be kidding! That was our sale of the week! We knew something was kooky there. What should I do? I was glad the gal had been so happy, but....

I complained, "That's $150 worth of clothes. I can't do that. I'll check with my accountant. We don't have that much money here to refund. My husband probably deposited it already. Come back tomorrow for an answer."

I doubt they expected that. So their sister was balmy; but to refuse a customer the right to buy if she had the money wasn't good policy. The sister added, "She should not have used her check that way. She escaped from the house and we want that money back." That line made me wonder. "Don't know when she'll be released from the mental hospital." The mental hospital could be their house. Did they still have her? Who knows?

They returned the next day for their money, and I explained, "I can't give you all of it; we charged 10 percent for the transaction, pressing the wrinkled clothes, etc." They seemed to think that was fair enough. We chalked that up to another Friday night bummer. Retail for you!

Layaways

Some stores didn't allow them, but we didn't mind. However, we sales-women wished to be warned when one certain family came in! After an hour of moseying around, asking prices of everything, they left leaving clothes on the counter and in the fitting rooms. Someone said, "Their ele-vators don't go to the top. The mother scowls and slumps, bossing those grown kids around. They're a problem!"

Lisa added, "You can see them with your eyes shut. I suppose you are also aware they need baths. The fitting rooms don't smell very fresh now, and I will spray them. Shampoos would help that stringy look."

Angela commented, "I won't dazzle you with my undeniable talent for news-gathering but I hear they've nothing to do, so stop at all stores to browse. Some turn them away after a while, because they like to layaway many clothes. They pay only when their welfare checks come."

I noted, "That figures, I'd call it the filthy rich. I've seen them fight and argue by my window. The old girl gets them in line, but they can't help some of that. I heard their mom exploits them however she can, and keeps the money. The last time they were two months overdue on their layaway, but paid up after I wrote to remind them. They tried to change items laid away, too. They argued with me about the letters: they have no phone, I guess. They are shifty, though no one claims the bunch pilfers."

"I'd just call them a family of bloopers. There's a man with them at times, married to one, maybe, and he seems to have a bit of common sense. Just keeps us on our toes, gives us something to do," Angela said.

"Too bad no one ever motivated them to use their time and meager skills in an appealing way, for them and society," I told Angela once. "They have poor self-esteem, thanks to their mom."

"That's one way of looking at it," Lisa finished.

Just then Gwen came in on her R and R break. We asked what was new. She said, "Our store will close permanently when Christmas is over. When the restaurant closed next door, we lost our heavy traffic flow. The dear landlords raised our rent two hundred dollars per month, and we've had it." What a sad tale. "The area will lose a tourist attraction and this build-ing will look worse then it already does with its black holes."

I felt sorry for them, knowing what the struggle is and was. I wanted to buy some of their hangings before they closed, maybe some Christmas pre-sents for friends. Just trying to help, so I laid some away myself.

Taxing and Subtracting

It was Friday night, dinner time, and Charles brought our tacos and drinks, filling our most quiet or slack period. What bothered me was that many people were only window shopping with the children, or checking for sales instead of buying. The electric eye was dead for an hour, though the last kids waited in the light to make it ping constantly. But what else was new? At least they didn't bump it off its hook or pull the hook out, chipping wall plaster and irritating Charles.

Another rule I learned before first grade was to share everything and play fair. While we were eating, I asked Charles to explain again what was taken from Angela's pay and other taxes he paid. With only one employee to figure, it was still a hassle, it seemed. If only family members worked for me, it would be simpler, but they had their own work to do. He used the calculator as he talked, and I had a review of the sharing philosophy, that is us, to the IRS.

"It is state income tax, federal income tax, and social security tax from Angela. I pay workmen's compensation, unemployment tax, sales taxes, city tax, plus insurance on everything, and an annual license fee to be in business. That's not mentioning the utilities, supplies, wages, or overhead costs. Good thing we don't have to pay an accountant. I use Brad to sketch some advertising, though I pay regularly to the media–and parking, don't forget. Many charities, legal and not so, call for handouts, too."

I moaned, "Where's our profit? Am I just working to transfer money from us to others? And we spend hours here and at home on records, ordering, inventory records, and repricing. We must like it enough to hang in there, or be too blind to quit."

Charles answered, "People have advised us to stay two to three years for a fair try; Lisa's alterations also cost, plus Brad's banners and signs. Imagine what the big stores upstairs spend. The scarecrows are the only workers that don't cost anything, and they get depreciated along with the other fixtures.

And to think we planned another store like this south of town when this one succeeds-if it does? Dreamers...."

Charles changed the subject. "Now let's consider some changes again, move goods around for effect. Oh, why don't you wear your name tag anymore? Al said you should, right?"

"I know my name! I am your significant other!"

"Now, let's not be testy," he grinned. "Let's go home or out for coffee?"

"Out for coffee to discuss the latest scoop–the head shop across the hall is closing at the end of the month."

Researching and Why

"Angela, what happened out there just now? I heard a commotion; why were people rushing and screaming?"

"You wouldn't believe it unless you saw it! The stairway was solid, railing to railing, with teenagers running and pushing up to the main floor. Must have been 100 yahoos; tough luck for anyone trying to reach our store, or the hair salon. Wow!" she exclaimed when I came from the back room.

"Did they come from next door or the back alley?"

"Next door, and two girls led them up, one the first half, the other the last. Could be spring fever already. I heard a man and his wife by our door a while ago say they were not coming back here. They don't like this noisy crowd of milling people. That's not good for our business. Just think of all who haven't told us that but think it anyhow."

"It's disgusting. Listen to the girl from the store at the top of the stairs." Angela went to the bottom steps to hear better.

"Oh, oh, there's been a fight in front of their store by that gang that just went up, blocking customers entering. Police are trying to break up the mob, but it won't move; they say it's a city street and they can stay there. That's bad for the mall's reputation. It's cold outside and the mall is a playground on nights and weekends."

I sat on my stool at the counter, feeling worse all the time. "I know, so noisy with the video game room next door; forty machines going ping, whoeee, whup, bing, rata-tat-tat, zap, boing, blam, beeple, blok, blip, bloop—and the boisterous banter or bickering of about eight kids, what can we expect? More security guards or signs must control it. I posted no loitering signs by the stairs and my door. The police check downstairs and trouble makers simmer down a bit, but disrupt when they go. A cop did remove two lippy ones."

Angela joined me by the counter. "They should. I'm sure you feel cheated and uneasy for your customers. I heard one lady ask, 'How do you stand that noise? Doesn't it get to you?"

I agreed. "I'm starting to hear the boings, beeples, and bloops in my sleep; it hinders my concentration when I'm here. It attracts loiterers who case my store and steal if I'm not watching. I've posted a sign ordering only two students in the store at one time because I can't catch them when they spread out or distract me. I don't like it."

She glanced at her watch. "Well, it's five o'clock, and I'm glad we're closed on Sunday. We need the rest."

"Sure do, and the gate next door is closing at six o'clock instead of nine or ten o'clock tonight, for a private party, I hear. Well, nothing's perfect. Angela, you know that the landlord won't allow us to break our lease before June, so we've got to endure this all spring? I think we'll search the mall upstairs for another spot. I heard of a corner store that's open where a men's store had been. But the price is more than double this one, and the necessary remodeling would cost a bundle, I'm sure."

"This became a lousy spot. On that note, let's go home!"

Robbed and to Court

I emphasize I am not a morning person, I think. Well, one morning, my breakfast was interrupted by a telephone call from a police depart-ment–the town of my store, no less–to inform me there had been a robbery there. "Contact us when you get here; we want to ask you some questions," I was told. What a predicament, enough to send me back to bed. On the way to town, I muttered to myself, "How did a nice grandma like me ever get talked into a job like this?" And I felt like praying.

The mall was not open upstairs so I came down the back stairs early, looking for a policeman. Outside my chain door, opposite the nearest clothes rack, I found the stick the thief used. I could imagine how he did it, pulling hangers of my women's pretty velour matching sweat suits through the holes and under the metal gate. With no one around to stop him or call the police, he took them upstairs.

I opened the door to let in the mall policeman I had just phoned to answer questions about the robbery. I reported what was missing. He told me, "The owner of the video game room saw the stuff on the floor as he was arriving and quickly called the police from a store farther down the mall. We caught the boy as he was leaving the mall with the suits. He dropped them to run, but we took him to jail. He was on probation and staying at the correctional center down the street. You'll be called to court to identify your merchandise, as will the game room owner to testify to what he saw."

Caught with the goods! That made me feel better! Later on the phone I told Lisa, "Our neighbor and I heard the judge today arraign the thief in court. We won't have to testify at the trial. He's guilty, caught by the police. They took pictures of our sweat suits for evidence so we can get them back." I added, "As I sat in court watching that poor boy, I wondered why he would break his probation for those few sweat suits. Wonder what he wanted women's clothes for?"

Lisa suggested, "Probably to sell to 'feed a habit.' Aren't people dumb?"

I'm learning to be a morning person, thanks to retail.

Prepared

There came a Saturday morning; Charles and I were fed up with Friday nights since the men came less than the women lately. What did they do? They picked over the stock for sale items or only bought as the season ended. Winter coats weren't selling-the weather had been too warm-so down jackets didn't sell either; that was what we had most of.

Then came Angela, the "Eye"; no one slipped by her, though kids tried *always*. She told me about the guys who watched from the stairs to see how many customers we had to keep us busy before they came in to shoplift. It was a battle of the wits between them and us. In the hall, the girls and guys were flirting already, making noise.

"Since it's raining," I said, "where else could they meet and play? Oh, this will be a long hard day for us. Let's take an early lunch break."

"Here's Charles. He's got a camera and a tape recorder with him, too," Angela noted, wondering out loud.

"Those are weapons of his strategy; we can't break this store lease, even though business fell because of the game room, so we're getting proof. We may have to go to court. Our lawyer checked the lease terms: 'A promise to have a peaceful place for business. Use that reason, he said. Look at that mob horsing around the steps and our door. That would make a good set of pictures, and it looks like he's got some. Great! Here comes the police!"

Angela glanced out the door. "Sounds like they're breaking up the gangs down the hall, too. The kids are asking who that man is taking pictures of them; they seem a little worried. Isn't this fun?"

"Sure is! The tape recorder is now tucked behind the fake palm tree by the counter, and catching all these raucous sounds. Never saw so much commotion. Oh, oh, it's the game room owner who's blasting a blabber-mouth kid, ordering him to leave. 'Never come back or I'll have you arrested!' That was taped too."

Angela noticed some girls pawing through the jeans and ordered, "Take only two to the fitting room" They had been sending their friends to the shelves for more to confuse her. I was glad we had the sign that limited two students at a time now.

Then we huddled. "There's the police again. What's going on? Our neighbor is using our phone, isn't he? What's he saying?"

Then my neighbor told me, "I've had it!" and called for more police from my phone. Uh, oh! He heard the tape recorder clicking near him! It had to be turned over! He stared at me, worried now. He left in a hurry, and saw Charles' camera too, so knew we were planning something.

Angela beamed, "Well, it's about time he realized we mean *business* here. His game room wrecked ours and he could be sued. Should have had adequate security all along."

"I know, I won't let Charles do it because I don't want trouble like that. It's hard enough to work close to the men every day without lawsuits, too," I explained. "We do chat together, they shop here, and he reported my gate robbery, even went to court to testify for me. We must move before June, which won't be easy. I'll bet no other business leases this for the remainder of that game room's five-year lease. What a day this turned out to be!" I walked away to think and wandered in and out of the fitting rooms.

"It's not over yet. Here's a lady from a shop on the second floor who wants you." Angela checked the back room for me. Finding me, she added, "Wonder what she wants." I walked to the front to listen to the stranger's stranger request.

"I want your spiral rack by your door with your skirts on it. It's mine, and was removed from my assorted supplies on the top floor of this building. It wasn't locked up, only piled with other things on the floor."

I was surprised, remembering the big mess up there. "I didn't know it belonged to anyone. My assistant, who's not working here now, said there were many discarded items up there, empty shirt boxes, old decorations, and brought it to me. You may have it back. He did paint it to match our decor. I'm sorry.

Then she looked around, and claimed the low, chrome one by the Elsie scarecrow, too. That thing had a broken foot, and wouldn't stand straight. I didn't care, really. Charles offered to take it apart to bring it to her shop. Why wouldn't people store useful items in locked rooms I wondered. Kent hadn't known they were not junk, so I couldn't blame him; she was happy. Me, too, as I also learned in kindergarten: Don't take things that aren't yours. Such strategy and wisdom we practiced that day!

Planning Each Step

We had become very flexible. For the first time we *emptied* shelves at the back of the store; we usually *spread* the stuff to make the store look *full.* I did not expect my spring goods early; I displayed each season's merchandise after the upstairs stores. Why did the shelves look so bare? We were moving! I checked three empty spots upstairs: a bank building, the store at the top of the stairs, and one by the mall back door. All were too expensive. About seven hundred dollars to three thousand dollars per month! The only other spot available was a mile from downtown, with too little flow. So we leased one across the street from the mall, a carpeted walk-in, only half our present size. I packed winter items slowly, as I told Angela, "To make it easier at the last minute when we must hurry."

"Why be in a hurry? That's a big job moving a store's inventory isn't it? When do we post a moving sale sign, like the one next door did?" she asked. This was exciting.

"I have two more months on my lease but we're skipping out early, since I can't get permission from the landlord. Our lawyer advised us to go without his knowledge, or he'd likely padlock the door and hold my stock till I paid all the rent. He did that to a restaurant upstairs, which could be a five-year case in court," I explained.

Angela laughed. "We're making a quick getaway? That's going to take planning so neighbors don't catch on. When?"

"On the last day of March, though that's two days before Easter, which is a loss of some Easter sales. Only two weeks away! The new store is being cleaned; I'm painting the walls later this week. That big clearance sale banner across the store is all the notice I dare to give. But did you notice the fellows from the game room stand by our door and watch us inside lately? Hope they don't suspect anything, or they'll tattle to the landlord. What a predicament! In a retail business, and we can't even take advantage of moving to draw people." I moaned, and added, "Charles suggested I finish the lease and quit. The slump hit us for two years, the rent doubles soon. I've enough reasons to leave this place; who says the other will be better? I told him, I think the outlet concept is still new, good, and improving in this town. My store name is better known now and people like my prices. Besides, sales were up the last half year, since the economy is turning. Moving eliminated many bad elements here, like upstairs storage, parking problems, public restrooms, poor air conditioning, useless elevator, inadequate signs upstairs for the public and it takes a lot of goods to fill this store. How would I sell all these winter clothes? These down jackets are a dud, thanks to a warm winter. Angela, you are a great help against shoplifters, and we get along so well. Our new landlady is a gem, compared to these birds. Liquidating is a big chore, I've heard," I rationalized.

"Well," she countered, "if it's half this size, where will everything fit?"

We'll be dropping the kids' line. But we'll be adding women's plus sizes, a new angle you know, and another type of customer to air our advertising. Mike Dida has pretty tops, bend-overs (pants), and coordinates for summer. He showed me at the spring show last week. Also, I'm contacting two other companies, one on the west coast, who have lovely, bright styles. The stout women asked me to stock their sizes, so what can we lose? The back room has lots of storage shelves, so no problem." I had an answer for everything.

"You think better months will come at a new location? You're accepting a challenge, I suppose. I hear Cissy also had added a new shop in another mall. Guess her business isn't too rousing here either. Her manager will miss us, I'll bet. She and I are good friends," Angela said, sadly.

"Cissy will, too. Her beauty operators, black and white, shop here. She's a young-looking grandma, and will be hurt if I don't warn her I'm moving because she said she liked me. But I can't tell anyone yet. She felt the effects of the game room, too. Bad guys wrecked her table and benches near the fountain which they plugged with trash. Oh, we're practical!"

Moving with Stealth and Flair

This was the magic day. Brad ripped out sections of shelves till late the night before and Lisa packed boxes with me after closing hours. All the winter clothes were stored in the nice, new back room already, so the plan today was to take the racks on one truck and clothes on another, as fast as possible. All the girls, their husbands, and Charles would work in teams, with another man hired to help.

The neighbors came to work, naturally, and stopped to ask what we were doing. The assistant next door asked, "Are you moving already?"

I answered, "Why not? Our new store is ready and these guys have time to help today."

Of course, I hoped he wouldn't tell on us! As fast as the boxes were being loaded on the freight elevator to the trucks out back, I figured we'd be done in one day. It was exciting and noisy. I liked it! The people walking by were looking at the new location sign posted outside the door, and Cissy stopped. She didn't look very happy, so I explained to her why we had to move. But she was a personal friend of the landlord, so how could I tell her ahead of time?

Angela announced, "It's raining a little now."

But that seemed to be par for the course with my business. All the shelves were down soon; since we had installed them, they were ours. Lastly, it was time for my scarecrows to move. Those young men of mine were not too gentle and Elsie's hair dropped off, with her hat thrown into a box. John lost his work gloves and toothpick, and Cecil his neck scarf, dude that he was. The males looked funny, lying or leaning with arms outstretched helplessly. What a mess the place now seemed to be; my neat store all gone! Still the eerie noises of the game room penetrated the walls and hall. I wouldn't miss them. We made it—no flak or delays from the powers that be! Angela kindly vacuumed the littered floor and carpet for us before lunch.

Kim's strong husband, Tim, and Brad, good and fast at constructing, caused a smooth transition. After a big lunch, my family went right back at it. All were having a good time—tired, but happy since the landlord never showed up. He'd probably sue, but that wouldn't be the first time, we knew. He didn't know Charles wanted to sue him.

There was a new wrinkle to this business: moving caused a change in decor from country store look to what? Painted creamy walls and ceilings, with dark rough shelves made no special impression-neat and tidy, yes. Do scarecrows fit? We kept the spool table for kids, one wagon for knits and socks, one bench to sit on for boot try-ons, but one wheel rack and a long rack would be left in the back room for extra garments. We sold one wagon to a florist and built a men's fitting room opposite two for women. A show window across the store front faced the street.

Life in a New Place

What would catch the public eye? Hmm, that wouldn't be easy. Fantasizing a bit, in the words of the now upright crows if they could talk, a solution crossed my mind.

"Now we're in this cold, back room and I want to be up front again, Cecil."

Elsie explained, "Give 'em time, John. They set us out of the way with our long arms, you know. Could poke their faces if they don't look where they're going. I can see it's a long store with carpets and a window; a narrow glass door opens at the end."

"Elsie, where are you? All these boxes block my view, more coming all the time. Now the empties are piling up."

"I'm out here in the store, John, in a corner by two fitting rooms. They empty cartons as fast as they can. The girls are arranging racks and clothes from the front to the back. I like this place, much lighter. Brad is nailing shelves on one wall; the other has a long peg board. Crows, wait till you see what's in the corner across from me!"

"What do you mean, Elsie? Something we'd like? We've new items back here. A white box as tall as us, with a door that opens when a light goes on–or does the light go on when the door opens, John? A fridge, I think it's called, for lunches and cold drinks, left here," Cecil piped up.

"Look at all these wood and metal shelves–to the ceiling–and a big cabinet with drawers, plus a work table, Cecil. Wonder what Elsie's got to show us."

"Besides two bathrooms and a work table, there's a lady with no clothes on. Someone set a hat on her thick black hair. And she's smiling right at me. John, is she ever pretty! You would like her, though she doesn't move or talk to people either. Our Lady is happy to have her; called her a mannequin–left here. She's more like a ladyquin, with her smooth, curved body. Wish I looked like that. I feel like a real hick now. Wonder what they'll use her for."

"No clothes on at all! Can't talk or go away, like us? Nobody got away with that where we came from."

"No doubt she'll have to display clothes, too. Or wear them maybe? Hangers couldn't hook on her, she's too rounded. She can't stand around like that all the time," Elsie said.

"Cecil, aren't you interested at all?" John inquired.

"She can't fit our decor, John, our country store look, remember? That's why they didn't want her type before. No, I'm not impressed, whatever she looks like. But I'll bet you my straw hat she'll stand in the window instead of us, and it's not fair."

"What a party poop attitude you have, Cecil. We've been a happy family till now, and we'd better keep it that way," Elsie scolded him. "I wish she'd talk to me."

"Now scrap boxes are either loaded on the empty trucks or some stored near the ceiling, Elsie. Means this moving job is winding down. Winter clothes are stored here so that's why this store has space enough, and I can see again.

"Crows, our racks are full, jeans and cords on the finished shelves. Clothes are sized as boxes empty. It's cold in here with the furnace off, poor ladyquin. I wonder what her name is. Charles said it should be Alexandra. Lisa is arranging this window with some of our same decorations: green chest, chicken clock, mottoes, and thorn wreath with mini scarecrow sitting on it–on the peg wall."

"Hey, Elsie, we're coming out. Now I see that ladyquin; Alexandra is a doll! I'm impressed! Among other things, that hair is what you lack for class, if you don't mind my saying so. Well, Cecil, may I ask your worthy unbiased opinion now? Great for our distinctive store, right?"

"Cool it! I don't want to be seen near her. She's perfect, I agree, but we don't need her! There's no room for us all out here with our long arms. I wonder how she'll stand alone, her feet aren't flat. She must lean on something."

John commented, "Looks like you're going into the window and aren't you lucky, watching the world go by. And she's going, too! I'll trade places with you; you're not compatible."

"Keeping her propped is a problem, I see. And how to dress her," Elsie said. "Oh, what a pretty pink blouse and print skirt on her–wish I had some new clothes. John, why are they undressing you? Your belly is falling down. Your hat, face, and shirt, are gone? They're using your skeleton to hold her up? Sure are! What a lovely gesture, giving yourself like that."

"For her, I'll do anything. Bye, Elsie, Cecil." So crow John was no more.

We realized we could be open before Easter after all. "It'll cost you to move," Charles admitted to me, "but it would be worse if we'd started a few days into the new month, since Easter comes at the beginning of it. Probably would need to pay a full month's rent, you know. So see what you can do here instead."

And we did attract some customers. Checking back to the old store, we re–posted our new location sign, which had either fallen down or been ripped off. And we advertised our new location via the media. We removed our logo from the hall to our wall just inside the door. Our cowbell hung on the inside of the door as a signal when someone entered.

The office buildings in adjacent blocks spilled out men and women during lunch hours and after work, many never knowing we existed. The idea of comparative buying took hold, we noticed, and many people checked our prices with those of a major department store across the street in the mall. We won out a few times, obviously, and lived such a peaceful life, as compared to our previous location.

Possibly a Crisis

A traumatic episode with Alexandra, the mannequin, could be fantasized a bit, like this, maybe?

"Cecil, now that we've occupied this show window together for a week and have an important job to do, are you going to stop this silent treatment and be civil? Your icy stares don't go with your silly smile. You're all bent out of shape because I'm gussied up and you're not, aren't you?"

"You're not my type, Alexandra; it's that simple, so let's drop the subject."

"Well, obviously, I'm the most 'talented pigeon in this dovecote,' so there! Seems I have entered the 'luxurious decline of my life.' "You are a person of dim importance.' Remember that! I heard those here before you came, I think. Don't answer me then. Here comes a mother with her brood to keep me occupied," Alexandra announced.

"Somebody help me! This little brat climbed in the window and is toppling me over! Cecil! Isn't anyone watching him? I'm falling on him!"

"Alexandra! His mom is near Elsie, I think. I can't help you. Let him break your fall, land on him. He'll learn!"

"Our Lady isn't a baby-sitter for customers, but I expect her to protect me. Cecil, this is terribly humiliating before all these people passing by! My skirt up to my navel. I'm heavy. Hear him whine? I've pinned him down. Oh, dear, I cracked my neck on his head and skinned myself, I know it. My lovely, slender neck is peeling. How long must we lie here?"

"Hang in there. His mom hears him and will help you. You scared him all right. You can't see his face, but he doesn't know whether to cry or not, Alex," Cecil noted.

"Oh, that feels better. That was a jarring experience. On my feet again and leaning against John." She smiled through her teeth as before, facing the street.

"Are you aware you're speaking to me, Cecil?"

"Well, that was an emergency. We won't speak socially."

"We'll see about that. Anyway, the boy is clinging to his mother." She said, "Glad she's not accusing me of falling on him. She could sue, I suppose, but *he* pulled my hand."

"Nobody saw him do it. People sue for slipping on ice *outside* of stores, you know. There they go, we're safe. He's obviously not hurting."

"Cecil, I'd say I tamed his spirit a bit."

Differing with the Boss

"Angela, I noticed when Charles comes in on Friday nights to help me he's always gung-ho. He looks the establishment over with those keen eyes and begins the interrogation. It's funny–here he comes." We watched him casually.

"Yes, he usually parks across the street so he has an objective view before he even walks in. If the front light isn't on, or marquee light, he makes a crack about it. He's smiling, anyway." She laughed.

"He's soft-spoken and direct, isn't he? He sits at the back table and reads the mail a while before he analyzes us."

Charles opened the door and said, "Hi! Where's the customers? I expected to see you gals running your feet off. You should have made a thousand dollars today."

I returned the fire. "What do you want us to do, corner them, get on our knees? We can't *make* them spend money."

"Well, you *know* it's location. You bought wrong and got wrong advice," he countered.

Angela looked at me as I answered. "Could be part of it, and some things are beyond my control. Don't make us feel worse then we do, *sir!*" I changed the subject and pointed at the hanging banner that was falling, "Please retie that." He was in rare form then.

"Why isn't that done? You had all day." That did it. I looked him square in the eye.

"I quit! I'm underpaid and handling money isn't my forte, which isn't news to you."

"Hold on! I'll give you a promotion; stick around."

"To what?"

"Oh, president of the company."

"With a raise?"

"Same pay, new title," he persisted.

"That's what I was afraid of." Angela had not been married so she thought this dialog interesting, I could tell. But he was not finished.

"Just think, you've a new wardrobe and your own car. It's nice getting dressed up with a flair every day out of necessity."

"Uh, uh. I'm handling two jobs, too, but I like it really. I only wish more people liked my goods, and I'm tired of trying to figure out why they don't. Angela says, 'That's retail!' And she ought to know." That settled that.

"Guess what, we won't repair things tonight after all." Charles relented. "Let's get some dinner. It's eight o'clock, so out with the lights, friends."

"Touché. Curtain, Angela!"

Charles' comments about poor sales due to lack of flow (customers) from bad location or buying wrong were like salt in wounds sometimes. Other times I could handle such criticism because I knew I was doing my best and should have patience to test that spot longer. He didn't know it, but I was never sure of any choice being wise. But on my way to work every morning, I said a prayer for help that day.

When the summer heat outside bothered people, I felt comfortable in my air-conditioned, cheery store and was thankful. I liked watching traffic go by, seeing the sunshine and meeting the neighbors in adjacent businesses. Life was not so bad, but that didn't pay bills, obviously. And Charles had that to face; his job supported us but this was not the case often for families in retail stores.

Finally, concern about making the wrong choice of location for a two-year lease settled in so deeply, I was desperate. Not that I could do anything, but I wanted relief. Who could tell me? No one knew. So I prayed for a sign to reassure me or give me the harsh verdict. Charles and I had bought a four-foot tall dieffenbachia plant some weeks before and placed it in our living room, but it was slowly dying, its leaves fading and drooping. That was a disappointment because it was expensive and not easy to transport home.

My sign was to have that plant revived soon if I made the right business move, or continue to die if I didn't. A week later the leaves began to turn bright green and perked up nicely. That was all I needed to push my feelings of failure away and put new life into my work. I told Charles, "Your doom and gloom forecast is not for me anymore," and I told him why. Of course, he pooh-poohed that sign, skeptic that he was, but I was satisfied for the present. Much later, that dieffenbachia outgrew its pot, hit the ceiling, and I took two large cuttings to pot for our girls. I never figured out why the leaves dropped tears thirty-six hours after I watered it. But with a name like that, why wouldn't it weep?

Understanding all Kinds

"Labels, brands, some folks live by them, don't they, Angela? That lady who just left, the hair and color coordinated blond, middle-aged one? Well, she scurried through the racks near me, asking, 'What labels do you carry?' I gave her a few. 'They're not my preference, not what I'm interested in', and left as fast as she could. Do tell!" I was a bit miffed.

"Some people swear by them. I suppose some labels are more true to their size; others tell their friends where and what they shopped for. I'm not impressed. Maybe we should be proud they condescend to come in here."

"Yes, our name is not synonymous with class, you know. Aren't we catty?"

Angela turned to me, standing behind our paneled counter, and exclaimed softly, "Oh, mercy on us. Note these two very large ladies. I

43

believe mom is the one with the glasses, with a plump daughter. I don't think we carry their sizes; 46 is the biggest, right?"

"Yes, in some things, not skirts and pants, just tops. I see they're choosing a few of each to try on, but they must be wishful thinkers," I answered. "And our stock would have to rise in size range, I believe, to supply them. I considered ordering to size 52, but decided too few are interested, so we can't risk it."

They left soon, but one seam had been split in a pants they tried on.

"Here comes a young man. He's not bad looking, but seems a bit unkempt, because his hair reaches his shoulders and I like the groomed look. So few men come in here, I won't be snooty." Angela greeted him cheerily.

"True, we get more older ones; no more little bored boys that whine. He could comb those ash blond locks and smile." I added, "Seems a trifle shy, now that I've listened to him answer your questions. He's that, or a man of few words."

Angela agreed. "He's a tall customer who sure seems fidgety. But he's trying on jeans and a western shirt, which look nicer than the duds he wore in, naturally."

Then he asked Angela, "Okay if I wear these out of the store?"

She answered, "Of course," as he came to the register to pay me. We both complimented him.

I said, "You look ready to go out on the town tonight." He wasn't very talkative, but then, we ladies were old enough to be his mother. He gave us a sale on a dull afternoon, thank goodness.

"Any ideas why we don't see Rose, your handicapped friend, anymore? She knows we moved, I'm sure," Angela asked.

"Yes, her mother won't allow her to cross the street alone; she can't see side view traffic. I stopped once to see her when I had time. Rose dropped in a couple of times after mass and phoned her mom from here, then I helped her cross the street. I miss her. In a way, we've lost contact with mall friends."

"Here comes a large man with his daughter, I suppose, though one never can tell. He's in a big hurry and so serious." I offered my services to him while he looked over the down jackets and jeans. I suspected we couldn't fit him, but showed him what was left, since our sale stripped us of good choices.

He blurted, "They're all wrong colors, jackets too plain, inferior."

"About now, we're not stocking many. We must sell all of them left from last winter first," I explained.

I may be wrong, but I thought his manner was distinctly male chauvinistic as he looked condescendingly at me. He dropped the jackets saying, "Let's get out of here!"

I showed one more in his size, which he missed. "I have this style you haven't seen." He left with a smirk; the girl obediently followed. That's retail.

Angela warned, "Oh, oh! The dingbat bloopers found us. I see they have the same old habits: inspect everything, ask a million questions, and lay-away a pile with the minimum down. But they paid for the tops they wanted and promised to pay for the remainder on time. I reminded them three times. We'll see."

Being Shocked

Sometimes I feared I had become a bit callused. Then I looked at the tiny lady ambling in. She was about 4'8", I guessed, so pale and wrinkled, but with a sweet smile. She wore glasses, likely a delicate grandmother. I watched her looking at small blouses, but supposed we had none for her.

"I like your puffy car coat with standup collar and maroon piping," I told her. The sleeves were too long, though turned up, showing maroon lining. I asked, gently, "Why isn't your coat buttoned in this bitter weather?"

She answered in a language I couldn't understand, or was it a thick brogue? I asked her to repeat herself. Did she say, "I'm small and maybe you haven't my size?"

"I have size five. What size are you? What do you need? Any pants?"

To which she answered simply, "Yes."

"Let me hold this five up to see. It's a bit narrow at the sides." Then she held a size seven brown pants with belt, like the five, and I showed her other colors. "Do you have time to try these on?"

"No, but I'll be back." She had pushed her white head scarf back a bit, and now drew it forward again.

I said, "It seems the seven is a better size. Do you need tops?"

"No, I have lots."

As she never answered why her coat was open, I still wondered. She should fasten it; she seemed so frail against the harsh November wind.

"I like your jacket," I mentioned again.

"I do, too. I got it last week. I broke my wrist." She held up her little hand. "I can't button it."

"Do you want me to do it for you?" I offered.

"Yes, it's cold out." I thought, *this poor thing*.

So I buttoned her snaps down the front. As she talked, I could hardly understand her. "I was hurt, slapped around and my hip, too, when I was thrown down hard," she stated.

"Did someone do it?"

"A big man knocked me down in my house and robbed me. Then he came back a second time and raped me," she answered in a calm voice, with a pleasant face, showing no anger.

What a shock! I did not believe that dear little woman at first.

"I showed him up in the mug books."

"Did the police catch him?" I asked hopefully, putting my arm around her.

"Not yet. I'll be back sometime." She headed for the door with a smile. All buttoned up, she was ready to go face the *cold, cruel world* again.

It made me want to weep for her. I almost did, as alone I sputtered, "It's not fair, not fair!"

Learning, Listening, and Layaways

I listened to the cheerful school teacher with me as she livened my afternoon. A plump one, with curly hair and quilted jacket. Attending school again, she said she wanted bargains. Her classes in communication caused her to say, "Everything is changing. People are blamed unfairly too often; children for poor respect for authority and parents for not training them; unions misunderstand management and visa versa. People must draw parties together more today. I never want to stop learning or trying new things." I agreed.

That was a switch from many of my customers who were disgruntled about minor things. I smiled and wished her well, she deserved it. Then another interesting customer entered, a young one with nice build, brown hair, and so friendly. Being diabetic, she temporarily wore an eye patch because her blood vessels hemorrhaged. The doctor in the next building cauterized them.

I remembered her, as she loved our styles and bargains, spending time to tête-à-tête with us. She claimed, "I can't control my diet well, so may eyes are reacting. My parents' menus are harmful, but I can't afford to move, and must eat what they offer." I became concerned.

"Can't you add a few sugarless foods for your mom to serve, or ask her to change the diet?"

"No, my dad wants his usual proteins and starches. It isn't good for her either as she's diabetic, too."

"I sure wish you could find a place to stay that doesn't charge an arm and a leg." I commiserated with her.

"I might move some day, I have a boyfriend out of town."

"We'll really miss you, but wish you well."

Angela agreed, then to me she complained, "Here comes a bunch we wouldn't miss. The Bloopers."

Then I agreed. "I had to write them again, they have no phone, a chronic problem. The oldest brought her letter to me demanding, 'What does this mean?' I told her, 'It means you must pay the balance and take the clothes out of layaway.' I'm too soft, allowing them to pay a little more until their check comes later in the week. I feel sorry for the kids, not the mom, who stays in the background, silent as a sphinx. I returned a shirt to stock as I told them I would. They mumbled and scowled."

"Don't worry about it," Angela said.

But later, I noticed my con artists went by, not paying as they promised that week, not looking in as usual, knowing they were overdue.

One day I knew that had to be the epitome of stalling. The bloopers showed their second letter to me. I ordered, "You must take your layaway now."

They looked at the sphinx, who shook her head.

"Those clothes go back in stock, though one item can go if you pay its balance," which seemed fair enough.

The short girl asked, "What do you want me to do, rob a bank?"

I answered, "I can't give you anything till you pay completely. It's long overdue!" They glared at my "injustice," mumbled together, and stalked out. My parting shot to remind them as they opened the door, "Your money cannot be refunded, it's our policy," brought no answer.

"I do believe we've seen the last of the bloopers in here. That's retail for you," Angela moaned, with a wink.

Burglarized and Aftermath

"Baby, it's cold outside!" came to my mind that day. Maybe that was why no one beat my doors down, either. The mommy leaving was the last of the big spenders as they say, and now it was dark, about time to end my business day.

Almost Thanksgiving, I thought, and after that everyone shops for Christmas. What a difference. They part with their money so easily, it becomes fun. The wives also do when hunting season opens, while their husbands skip town. But this year? Wasn't like the other store.

A customer entered in a hurry, bundled up good, ski mask and all, though his face showed. He asked me nothing about our clothes. "Did a young woman come in with long black hair and a pretty face? I was to meet her here." He seemed nervous.

"Well, we had none like that all afternoon," I answered.

He left quickly; he was tall, slender, average looking, though his eyes seemed heavy-lidded, a sullen look. I had a letter to finish. I wanted to mail it to a friend that night, as she had problems, possibly needing encouragement. So I wrote at the back work table till I heard the doorbell and recognized the same young man.

He yelled to me, "I found her next door!" Why? Do I care? But he did not leave, though I turned again to my letter.

When I looked up, I saw him running fast toward me. I asked, "Do you want help with something?" He didn't answer. His eyes were wide, dark, and menacing. He *struck me* in the face and *knocked me* hard to the floor! My glasses flew under the table.

He glared at me. "Are you alone! Don't look at me!"

"My...my husband is back there!" I pointed to the back room, wishing that he were. He planned to come in early for his new glasses, from the store behind our parking lot.

He spoke low and firm, "We'll go back and see."

He pulled me up, but I warned, "God is watching you!"

He opened the door, "I know." I called, *"Charles! Charles!"* but I knew he was not in yet.

The man saw the darkened back room and ordered, "Lie down...on the floor! I'm going to tie you up."

From the back room doorway, he noticed my vacuum attachment cord and tied my wrists with the shorter one, not too tightly, I noticed. He repeated, "Don't look at me!"

But he scowled at me lying on the cold floor, with those bug-eyed pupils staring, so I answered, "I'm not!" and shut my eyes. I realized then what was happening and was afraid. I repeated, "God is watching you," to reassure myself, too.

"I know it! I don't want to hurt you, I want your money!" My left pelvis and face really hurt by then.

"Take it!" He asked for my purse. "In that box by you on the shelf."

He dumped out everything on the back table and opened my wallet. I said, "I've only five dollars." I heard him open a pack of gum and chomp on a stick like a little kid. "Why are you doing this? What did I do to you?" Something seemed familiar but not his voice. It was stern and low.

"Don't look at me," he insisted. "Lady, you've more than I do, I want it. How do you open your cash register?"

I explained, "The lower right button," but knew it wasn't so. I decided to stall him, hoping someone would come in. I heard him tip over my tote bag setting on a chair, and warned, "There's no money there."

"I'm going to cover you so you can't see me." He dumped it over my head. While he was up front, trying to empty the cash register, I shook off the tote and began to untie my hands. I planned to rush out the back door to the office next door. I heard the "ping" of a wrong key, saw him in the distance, but by the time my hands were free and I stood up, he had run back and saw me.

"I told you to lie down. So, you are loose!" Now he was angry.

"I can't lie there, it makes me dizzy. I had to get up, I'm sick." I really felt awful, also from my arthritis in my right buttock. Then he tied my ankles and wrists again, tighter this time, with both vacuum cords and sat me down hard. He replaced the tote bag.

"You'll suffocate me! Let me breath!" I pleaded. But he said, "No, I don't want to hurt you, don't look at me. If I told you I was going to rob you, you would have laughed at me." I heard nothing for awhile, but hoped someone would see him under store lights with a ski mask on, running around. Then he returned with the register which I heard him set on the table, pushing aside supplies. He took the tote bag from my head and ordered, "Now open that register!"

"I can't walk there, my legs are tied too tight."

"I'll carry you!" I hated that thought! I decided not to cooperate, I was so angry at the humiliating experience. He carried me to it, and in the darkness, I pushed a few wrong buttons. I sensed his impatience when I saw a long stick waiting over my head. He threatened, "I'll give you five seconds to open it, *or I'll hit you!*"

I opened it; he moved me back, covered my head, and scooped up all the cash he could get. "There's more than this. Give it to me."

I denied it, "We've had some bad days lately!" I feared more torture, and was glad he believed me.

"You stay here while I take a couple of your down jackets and leave by the back door," he ordered.

And I said, "I'll stay." I was hot under the bag but sensed him too close to trust, so I waited for him to return to pass me for the rear door. It was quiet; I dreaded getting up to face reporting, identifying, whatever was ahead. Let me die. I heard the door bell. I wondered if a customer entered; he'd have to hide. I should yell. When no sound came, I knew he had left instead.

I shook off the tote bag and got up, but couldn't reach the phone. Leaning forward and seeing nobody, I yelled for the girls next door to help. I couldn't walk or crawl because of the vacuum's weight. Finally I worked my wrists loose, then my ankles, knowing time was wasted.

The girls looked in my window, not knowing what to do. I motioned for them, and they listened as I gave details to the police dispatch operator with a description of the thief. One girl brought ice for my bleeding, swollen lip and cheek.

Then police arrived, asking more questions; answers further relayed on the phone were interrupted by a long distance call from Charles still at *home*.

I moaned, "Where are you? I've been robbed and can't talk now, police here are questioning me. Hurry!"

More police drove up, what a commotion! The girls left, one in tears for me. She admitted she was afraid for themselves next door. One detective dusted for prints; the other had the identification kit for a composite likeness for me to identify. Dazed, tired, I tried to think. When would it end?

Another police car and officer. He already had a yellow ski mask for me to identify? I thought it was the same, though I couldn't understand how it was found so far away. It was dim in the squad car, how could I be sure?

Charles finally arrived. He looked concerned for me. I told him in the back room, "That did it! I can't take anymore. It's not worth it!" More police trooped in. Why?

"We are waiting for the print man to finish," they said. "We're all going on a hunting trip this weekend and want him to hurry." I heard more questions.

"How much do you think the thief took?"

"About two hundred dollars. He said he'd take down jackets; seemed like an amateur, but I'm no authority on that. Maybe on drugs."

All the fuzz had left. It was like a tomb in there! Typically, we cleaned up his mess in the back room. We would never be the same again. I knew my spark abruptly disappeared. I heard Charles say, "We'll be late to the barter group trade auction," but I was not interested. "We have to eat," he reminded me.

"I can't open my mouth-maybe soup?"

At dinner, such as it was, Charles quipped, "You'd better close your store and write a book on how *not* to have a successful business."

It hurt to laugh, but I said through the side of my mouth, "I've already started," and pointed to my forehead.

A man waited in his car in front of the store next morning. I wondered why, suspicious already. I came a bit late, but made it. He followed me in with two huge books-mug shot books. Showing his badge he said, "Detective Parks, how are you?"

"I didn't sleep much, but I'm okay." Brad came in and I introduced them. Then to the books; what a pain. I had to note each picture carefully. How frightful to think all those crooks were on the loose, scads of them. None seemed to match my memories, however.

I admitted, "I'm not much help to you on this. These few look somewhat like him, but without a ski mask on, it's hard to tell." I fingered a frame around some faces, trying to get perspective. "Will he come back again, do you think?"

"I don't think so. I have some good news. Last night, a man waiting in his car for his mother in the back parking lot saw the robber at your rear door, before robbing you. He can identify him. Your size descriptions match." A relief!

"The ski mask they found wasn't the same after all; I remember another color of trim around the face holes. Also my husband and I are going away for a few days, to Canada, if you expect to reach me." Then he left.

Brad waited in the back room till then. He kept me company over cof-fee, gave moral support, plus ad advice. My jaw ached, as did my buttocks when I sat down. Retail, bah!

Being Sympathetic

I called Angela and described my experience the night before. She was sympathetic, but I sensed her throat tightened as we talked. She spent hours alone when I took my day off, or ran errands, so I understood her new fears. The newspaper gave a brief account of the robbery, including what was taken, which I resented. The police suggested I remove my scarecrow, Cecil, from the window for a clearer view from the street. He was relegated to the storage area and held extra or off season garments.

A pleasant-looking couple looked around a while in the store, fingering jackets and blouses. They were not serious shoppers, I could tell, when they approached me at the counter and began discussing my lot as owner today. I surmised they knew of my robbery.

They told me, "We live in this neighborhood and have been robbed at home. One time, we came in from the car and two young men were grabbing things from our drawers. They ran out the door when they saw us, so I followed one and almost caught him. He did drop some of my stuff, but he had not been caught, though I know what he looks like." He sighed.

That did not encourage me very much. I said, "I hope that nerd slips up somewhere and is nabbed. I watch for him every time I'm in the mall."

Then the lady told her story to me, in a soft voice. "Not long ago, while grocery shopping I was observed, because when walking home a mugger knocked me down hard from behind and took my purse. I hadn't seen anyone near me in the store. He took my credit cards, license, and money-all gone. I hated the inconvenience and the groceries were spread all over in the dim light."

I thought, what a sad way to live, with fears and harassment like that. Poor people. Troubles are a way of life! They meandered out; my blazers didn't fit him, nor were any of the blouses the right color for her. It helped me to share hurts with customers who understood, but not to mention them to anyone else. I also took heart, if possible, in the fact that most people knew we retailers were sick and tired of being ripped of by shoplifters and thieves to the tune of billions of dollars every year.

I had told Angela, "I believe it's for my good these bad things happen, but I must be patient to see how." And the next day I was tested again, and by a person ever so different.

Panicking

I caught a good look at a weirdo who came, and I froze. I could see clearly he was up to no good, and kept my eyes on him: Tight black pigtails stuck out from all sides of his wide brimmed black hat. Why was he wearing shades on a dark day? He was *spooky!*

He walked so slowly toward me. I just stared at him as he came closer and closer! I finally asked, "Do you want anything in particular?"

"No, just looking."

Afraid, and being alone, I wondered whether or not he was trying to be funny in that costume, or what? Probably wants to shoplift; I think I need the police visible. I backed up to the phone and then he asked, "How much are the men's T-shirts?"

"A dollar fifty." I did not expect him to buy any, so I stayed on that phone, a call to Lisa. I wouldn't go near him. I could hardly talk, numb on the spot. I muttered to her, "Go ahead! I'm too scared. He's such a creepy looking guy, I can't put the phone down!" I clicked the receiver but clutched the phone till I saw a police car stop before the store.

A big familiar sergeant came in and showed me his drawings of the night of the robbery. What timing! He did not hurry but made it a social call. I wondered how he reached me so fast, if he was answering the call Lisa made for me. He watched the weirdo and started to talk again.

"How was your vacation? Did you have a good time?" He was the one who had told me to try to get some sleep after the robbery, a very nice man. I glanced, relaxed now, at the fascinating bum, thinking the atmosphere had become a bit charged by then. Would he feel compelled to make any meaningful gestures soon? Then he did.

He dropped the underwear to the pile and slowly walked out the door, though no one bothered him. I smiled and told the officer, "Thanks so much for coming! You sure helped my adrenaline go down. Seeing him come toward me like that was too soon after the thief did it. I froze and called my daughter. She insisted on calling police to have you visible."

That policeman understood me! He stated, "I saw him going into your store and was waiting for a call, expecting to chase him for shoplifting or something. He looked the type. Well, now that he's gone, you'll be okay. I chatted casually so he wouldn't think you called for me. We've been watching your store more but can't be here all the time," he reassured me.

" I know that. I wish we could afford security."

"You know, when the store my wife worked at was robbed, she couldn't stand to go back, so she quit. Gets to you."

I thanked him again, and he sauntered out. A week after the robbery and still so petrified. I sat down on my stool and could have cried from weakness. A hero I was not!

Conferring

Later, Angela and I had a serious chat at the counter. She pulled up a chair as no customers were around. We reviewed the turn of events in the store, even discussed my deep feelings about the robbery.

"I had time to think and pray while on the floor that night. What would he do to me? I remembered that tiny old lady who had been in three days before with a broken wrist, robbed at home and raped. I thought of the older women alone in the world, who live with that fear all the time, and I sympathized-and became angry. When I heard him chewing my gum from my purse, I thought, I'm old enough to be his mother. What was his mom like, that he would strike me in the face? Afterward I was too weary to get up and call the police, and I hoped it was all a bad dream. I just wanted to die. And now I fear he may come back because he might think that mask found so far away, as the newspaper account gave, throws the investigation off. He'll always need money if he's on drugs, I didn't tell all that to the police."

Angela knew I had to get it off my chest, to quote a cliché, so she was quiet and listened. I admitted, "Well, I have a hand alarm in my pocket now, so I should not be afraid of anyone. It blasts a loud buzz." I demonstrated it. "I'll leave it here for you when you are alone. We should plan tactics now. I'm worried about you being alone, too, as the paper announced two hundred dollars was taken. Any jerk who wants some cash might rob us again. I'm sorry they mentioned that and I wrote that to the editor. Also I included an article I hoped would help correct the general situation for us women, but they won't use it. The gist was something like this:

"Women, to understand their God-given role to influence their children and husbands, be respectful to them and others; to report spouse abuse and any thief they see around."

"Men, to teach their boys that both sexes are equally important, and be a good example. They can urge the young to watch and care for the helpless women they see, defend them."

"All, can report and help prosecute crime; then expect the guilty to repay their victims, with assigned duties from their court trials."

Angela tacked reassuring verses from the Bible on the counter edge, adding, "They're to give us more faith each day." Then free books and Bibles displayed by the door, for "Year of the Bible" emphasis, were picked up often.

Angela vowed, "We gals will not give up yet; let's plan to watch our signals together. We're not to discuss this robbery with people. It could drive customers away in fear."

"True!" And we had another cup of coffee.

Dropping and Promoting Lines

Shortly after, who returned but that same weirdo late one morning. I wondered, What's he want? Why doesn't he work? Keep your eyes peeled on him again. Of course, some people are famous for not going to work—it takes a lot of planning. This time he dressed less obnoxiously, no pigtails, and he left his sunglasses home, though the sun was shining. Probably off his high so he could handle bright light.

He stopped at the shelf of men's underwear again, but I didn't follow him. I ran a self-serve store for his ilk now. He asked, "Do you have this in small?" and held up a pair.

"Only what's there; we're out by now, I'm afraid." I had made the decision to close out the men's department after the robbery and not order anything, even for Christmas.

You could count on your hands the men who shopped in a week, and most usually were the wrong size for my goods. I knew in retail, you reason just the reverse. We should have every size and color, or the word gets out. "They don't have anything." Was he buying, casing the place, or what? He'd been back there too long, in my opinion.

But finally he came forward with one T-shirt. Big sale! About the cheapest thing in the store. The last of the big spenders, like many other suspicious-looking characters we had lately, the silent type. Often as they stared at me, I was uneasy. Were they trying to wear me down? Or don't their elevators go to the top? I watched him walk slowly down the street like a zombie.

Later that week, I was to give a Total Woman speech again, and show coordinating styles for reducing women to help them dress attractively. Though they were still heavy women, or adjusting to smaller sizes and sacrificing their favorite foods, an attractive clothes look compensated. Literally, their diets took the starch out of them.

It was a lot of heavy work to pack or bag what I set aside. The last time I demonstrated for an out-of-town show, I sold only four pieces. The style shows really had not paid off. But I was willing to try one more time, because of my many attractive plus sizes. And business had been nothing to write home about. December or not. I hoped the weather would not be nasty when I transported all of it.

A pleasant, extroverted lady had read my and Angela's handwriting at the store a few weeks before and asked for the style show and speech. She liked our styles and lines, "Just what we need for encouragement these days," she said. She had read some of our personality traits right, but Angela figured that was typical of many people. And I liked what she had revealed to me. Oh, well.

I would offer a style show at the store, using the long aisle with guests sitting near it, but supposed promotion could cost a bundle and the typical December shopper was too hurried for such affairs. I mentioned to Angela the idea of trying a special kind of show where you show nine to eleven pieces that can be matched enough to form a whole wardrobe. Lisa and I considered it, but we were too apathetic. Since the robbery I'd lost interest; I still had my sore hip and cheek bones, and was so tired. I watched everyone carefully, especially some young guys who cased my jacket rack too often. Not able to afford extra help, I stayed to the front of the store more than before, with my hand burglar alarm always in my pocket. Such is the retail business!

Being Alert

Coming back to work after my day off, I found Angela excited about something strange she had noticed the day before. She blurted, " I saw a young man furtively staring at me through the front window. I recognized him as that one who bought a western shirt and jeans and wore them out of the store, quite unusual. He acted nervous, remember? And spoke as little as possible. We were pleasant to him and there was nothing to warrant the *guilty* stare he gave. He saw me watching him, so he quickly crossed the street, looked back at our sign above the store and at me still observing him. He knows our store's name. Could he be the thief? He fits your size description, right?"

I agreed, "Yes. What if he was? Could I be sure? Unless he had a police record and we could see his picture and know his name. I didn't find it last time I looked. I'd like to examine the mug books again," I said intensely.

Angela affirmed we should. I called Detective Parks. "He's bringing other books tomorrow, Angela. Don't hold your breath, but here's hoping I get a break. You made my day!"

Enter Detective Parks–ta da!–with four more mug books. What a hassle to search all those, I figured, but we viewed them slowly, discussed a couple, and rejected them. Oh, oh! I exploded, "Look at this, Angela! Those heavy lids, long hair, the slight smile of the man who bought those clothes."

Angela agreed, "Sure is, I can tell that profile is the same as the one who watched me two days ago. What are his statistics?"

Parks read them. I remembered, "He weighed 154 pounds, he is 5'11" and in his mid-twenties! Why is he in that book? Probation of a drug charge? Really, Detective Parks?" Then it dawned on me. "*He* did *that* to me? Is that why he said, 'If I told you I was robbing you, you would have laughed at me.' What a relief! I don't want to accuse the wrong man but that's him." With that the detective left and we were beaming. But what next?

"Wouldn't they question him about an alibi that night? Maybe put him in the lineup for me to identify? I don't know much about such things,

Angela." I noticed his name, Mickey Page, and told Angela, "I have friends with that name, who have boys his age. Now I'm worried again!"

"What a predicament!" Angela agreed.

The next time we chatted after she had worked alone, Angela had additional tidbits to tell me. The plot was thickening, it seemed, and we had to keep up to date. She began, "I got a couple of squirrely young guys here, so I stayed up front. It looked like they were trying to corner me–about the same age as Mickey. I was alert and skeptical. Why do they want help with *little girls'* coats, which one looked at? The other pawed through *infants' sleepers*, trying to draw me there. They were fidgety and eyed me too much for comfort," she professed. I wished she could be spared such worries.

"I became more suspicious of them, too, because the one by the sleepers asked me, 'Are you connected with the clothing store next door?' You know the beauty shop that features a clothes boutique? 'What do you mean?' I acted innocent. 'The store next door, is it part of this one?' "I headed for the door, and said, 'Show me!' He followed me, while he pointed to the hair salon, I answered, 'No.' I waited for his buddy to come out. Thank goodness! They were testing me. They crossed the street. If I must say so myself, that was a neat and easy trick; I won't forget them."

I put my arm around her shoulder. "That was tricky. It could have been bad news and I'd say you are playing a great detective act, Angela! You are an angel."

Getting Acquainted and Sharing

The affable neighbor who had been waving to us so often finally came in. He owned the shop on the corner. Angela knew him well and said he had retired, but couldn't stay home and do nothing. She greeted him cheerily, "Hi, Hank, it's about time you stopped to chat; you aren't that busy, you know."

He stamped the snow off his feet, smiled, and answered, "I know, but I'm out walking for exercise and can't get it if I stop here. How's business? Heard you had a robbery. Did they catch him?"

"Not yet, but we identified him." He lit his cigar, obviously an exception to our no smoking policy. His glasses steamed a bit from the cold air.

"That's good. Hope they get him. I'm tired of all the pointless compassion for the criminal. We're out of the way and have to watch these bums, too, but we always have more than one clerk in the store."

Angela admitted, "We can't afford it all the time. We do now for Christmas sales. Stop by again!"

"It's cold outside; this visit took the edge off. Thanks."

We noticed him to be a short man who was not aggressive, different from some such customers we knew. Angela drawled, "One can never tell by looks. Now take little Betty; she's short also. An example of a faithful cus-tomer-employee from a store around the other corner. She buys our new frilly, feminine styles on her way to the bank. She's worried her boss will wonder what keeps her away so long, but they're not busy now. For being seventy years young, she's very pretty, with lovely gray hair."

"Yes, I agree."

"She's been my friend for years," Angela added. "She checks our skirts or pants quickly and puts a favorite on layaway. She has to try them on after work, or she drops by on her lunch break. She's good advertising for us, likes our inexpensive items and dealing with the public, she tells where she bought them. So she and others from there love to go to the bank and scan what we have." Angela picked up the phone to make a call and I put water on for coffee.

I straightened the socks, mittens, and gloves while watching a little bar-gain hunter to beat all hunters. She would try on everything and like the opinions of us saleswomen. What a happy grandma, with not a hard figure to fit. Middle-aged with graying hair, she bought in bunches when she found clothes she liked. She took a while to decide, though; a bit like me. Probably had to be a bit of a penny pincher.

Angela informed me, "Her daughter is just like her. Those grandkids are something else."

I mumbled, "Yeah, they think they own this place."

"You're right, they just traipsed into both bathrooms without asking."

"Really? Those aren't for public use without permission; I hope they flush. I'm not about to clean bathrooms after store hours." I then added, "Well, nobody's perfect. Grandma's a proud mom and happy wife. She just phoned her husband, who seems special to her. Good communication, as our teacher friend would say." Angela sipped her coffee without comment.

After I heard the cowbell blink and saw them all mosey down the side-walk, I said, "Which reminds me, parents who come here are usually good and concerned about their young. A daddy conversed with me about the problem teenage boy with him yesterday. Seems he couldn't please him and felt so badly about it. I told him to not give up, the phase would likely pass, as I remembered from my own experience. He was wise, and didn't give in to the demands of the insolent guy by paying for the most expensive blazer he chose. Bully for him! I don't need that sale."

Judging the Signs

"The store looks nice for Christmas, Angela. The tree lights blink so brightly in the window, and the big red and green banner Brad hung across the store wishes holiday greetings. With the weather good for shoppers, sales are steady. Alexandra's party dress looks lovely; I like having a mannequin to dress up. I expect her to look pretty and stylish. When I hear women ask about her and her clothes, I'd like to say flippantly, 'Put your money where your mouth is and buy it!' Of course, I don't dare. Many are only browsers, I know."

"You know, a jumper or something to cover Elise's droopy pants might attract interest in her robe rack; robes are good Christmas items," Angela reflected.

"You're right, I don't know why I don't think of a change for her appearance. Maybe I take her for granted.

"But go ahead. Look around for anything unusual. Doesn't that music cheer you? Does me. The sweaters and holiday coordinates brighten the women's department nicely. Did you know half of that order didn't come through? Angela, I got cold feet, but threatened to beard those suppliers in their dens. It was too late when I realized no more stock was coming. The suspense of not knowing how much of any order will arrive, and when, kills me," I complained. "I advertise, expecting new goods to display, then can't. Sales are down from last Christmas at the other store."

"How about your pre-holiday sale flyers, with discount coupons for preferred customers?" Angela fingered a bit of mail from a supply company.

"So few sales came from my mailing list, I wonder why I sent them out. They cost me time, and the printing fee. Even postage for a thousand names shocked me, so high. I hope to try again next spring, though. The last one, two Christmases ago, paid for its cost only, through sales. Maybe flyers aren't as good as radio. I can't decide what is the best means to promote anymore. Charles tries all of them now that the billboard lease is finished. He's taking his cue for the future from this month, he said. My ESP isn't working, I guess." A lot of holiday spirit I demonstrated just then.

"To change the subject, we never did hear from the police about finding Mickey, did we?" Angela questioned. "Who knows whether or not he's spying now to ransack our till again."

"Don't mention that depressing subject, Angela. Keep your chin up."

She glanced toward the ceiling, laughing. "Oh, I will. If I hurt on the inside, it won't show. We have an image to maintain, you know. It's beginning to look a lot like Christmas!" she warbled.

Deciding a Course and Planning

My lack of a Christmas bonus didn't break my heart or spirits, just my will to go back to work in a northern winter. I parked across the street; the snow was too deep to open the back door of the store. Oops...I almost slipped, trying to climb the high snow bank at the curb (plows do that), obviously not thrilled with it all. Thankfully, Angela was due later. This was the week of markdowns and exchanges, so we would need enough money on hand for refunds, but no fears with both of us there. So cold in that barn with the heat off for three days! I touched the thermostat and waited a while. I figured Christmas decorations could last a couple more days. The happy time of year was over for awhile–dead time–enough to put us in a funk?

Some have a motto. "Be nice to them when alive; ignore them when dead." If many customers thought my demise was coming, it could apply to me. I had to see what things looked like with lights on again, so I flicked the buttons. Angela, bright and smiling, came in. She could cheer me up. We told about our holidays and I heated water for coffee. She had brought big raisin rolls to eat with it, so that was our first order of business. I loved her!

Then our first exchange, ma'am! I noted her bag–interesting. Turned out she merely needed a bigger size of an oxford cloth shirt for her teenager. What do you know? We had her size and the color she liked. That was too easy; back to our chit-chat–serious, that is, *very!* I told her, "Charles decided just last night to sell the business if he can. If not, he'll have to liquidate everything. It seems he's not getting adequate return on his investment. Our clothing stock sources are 'drying up,' as he put it. He's not making enough money to suit him, as more outlets have started now, also."

Angela understood perfectly. "Lots of businessmen make that decision," she admitted.

"Who says life is stable?" I asserted, "He'll advertise it first. We ladies must mark down *everything;* 'slash it!' he ordered, 'and see how much you can sell the next three weeks. Then reduce prices with a greater percentage every couple of weeks.' This week our ad read, Clearance Sale on Everything. Our work *starts now!* Did I say that? What did I *do all this time?*" I stared at her ruefully.

"No wonder you feel miserable. You struggled to have a successful business and career. You like people and made many friends here," she empathized.

"Apparently it's over! We can't afford two sales people here in the January slack time ordinarily, and I'm a bit afraid when I'm alone, you know. Driving weather this time of year is an unpredictable pain, too. I'll need you full-time for sales." I put my arm on her shoulder.

She smiled, "I'm glad we have much work to do, so I'd say we should get busy."

We wondered what happened to Mickey. Angela suggested I call Detective Parks. I did. "Hmmm, what do you think about this? Angela, no one did *anything* because the police were busy checking out the new holiday robbery cases. They will let me know. That's not a good sign, is it? A stall?"

"Oh, no, there's lots of crime at Christmas, and fights and accidents. Patience is the word to remember now. At least you don't have to choose him in the lineup while your closing is on your mind," she reassured me.

"The saying, 'Christmas is the season that makes or breaks retail stores' sadly fits mine, but I won't have to sweat it again–unless someone buys this and wants us lovely ladies to remain, Angela." We looked skeptically at each other.

"Cased"

There's a theory that's true, no matter how old you are. When you go out into the world, it is best to hold hands and stick together. Angela and I did when we could.

"My, what a breezy character he is. I've never seen him before but he acts like he belongs here," Angela said quietly to me. He said hi to her as he strode to mens' jackets and blazers. "Keep your eyes open!" she added.

I moved back via the wall aisle. For starters, he looked at me strangely, full in the face, while I was busy with another customer. He was about the height of Mickey, fair skin and hair color, too. Possibly a relative? Rather gutsy, he asked me, "So you're going out of business. Why?" as though he'd heard about me and my store, or I owed him an explanation. His smirk got to me and I stared back at his severely blotched face. I didn't answer. Then to Angela he said, "I saw it in The Shopper."

I sensed he didn't sound like one for us, so must be casin' us. He tried on down jackets and a couple of fiber fill samples. "I'd take this if one of you pretty ladies would put the price down."

What nerve! I blurted, "No way!"

He picked out more and pumped Angela, "When are you closing? What are you going to do? Where are you going, if I may ask?"

She was sharp, "You may ask but I won't tell you, because we don't know yet," she said.

Good ol' Angela! Then he said in his know-it-all tone, to my customer, "The one you picked is not down." But the customer didn't care. He liked the price. While at the men's underwear shelves, he asked Angela, "Can I try on a pair of these boxer shorts? One has a flaw."

She told him, "It's against the health rules." But he stalled there so long.

I watched him from the counter as Angela came to me to confer. "I'm suspicious now," she whispered. "Remove some money from the cash register." I did, to a shelf below where I hid it. As she left me, she announced forcefully, "I'll use the back phone."

I stated, "okay," loud enough for him to hear. I saw her faking a call to the police, while observing our nerd. He eyed her and heard her say clearly, "I'll see you in a minute." He put down a navy jacket so fast it'd make your head swim, and headed my way with pink leg warmers–womens'–you couldn't miss the hot pink!

Next he asked me as I rang them up, "When are you closing? What are you going to do?"

"We don't know yet." He was zany. He dashed to his car out front and roared away.

I told Angela, "I'm marking down the flawed shorts to seventy-five cents. I'll never forget that face. These young guys are acting so sneaky lately."

"Well, we remember they did at the other store too, so what else is new?" Angela affirmed.

"Too bad someone doesn't punch them in the nose. Scratch that, in the nursery school sandbox we learned not to hit people. Very elementary, huh? Nobody dares fight back today, not that way, at least. You'd be sued. But I saw clearly, we were cased just now."

Confronting the Enemy

Is there a saying, "I see the enemy and he is us?"

I'd seen this customer before and I didn't like him, I didn't think! Why? Just an ordinary-looking guy, but a bit familiar. I remember–it was the way his head turned when he entered, his walk, his body build reminded me of someone. I slowly approached him from my back area, and asked, "Do you need my help?"

He answered softly, "I'm just looking."

I turned rapidly to the back table phone, dialed Lisa, and talked so low she could barely hear me. But I was desperate! He looked at the men's boxer shorts not far from me, and I glared at him all the time while talking. I heard myself say, "No, it's *him!*" That meant only one person: *Mickey!* She knew! I asked louder, "Is he coming in soon?" I meant Brad, but said nothing much, mumbling. Helpless, too scared! Too nervous! "Okay, yes."

Hang up? No! No! I merely clicked the hook and clutched the phone receiver harder. I knew if he heard me give an address, he'd probably run out or attack me. I wondered if the police would come. She would call, I knew. I stayed back, though gibbering, while Mickey walked toward the front counter. He stopped at the mens' blazers, listening, I supposed. He went to the cash register with the shorts, gazing out the window. It was him, all right.

Ah, some customers! Not alone anymore! I could not go near the cash register otherwise. Some moms and their girls gave me lots of witnesses. He didn't talk at the counter, but I inspected the shorts. "These have a flaw, that will be $1.82 for the two." I glimpsed at his face while he put his change in his wallet. A calm, cool character, walking straight as you please to the door.

Oh, great! The police pulled up! They got out and looked inside at me.

I nodded toward Mickey. They talked. What timing! I helped the customers then, though shaky as could be. They wanted to browse, and the kids poked around the racks. Horrors! The policeman and Mickey came back in!

The policeman asked, "Is this the one?" Those customers watched.

I affirmed, "I feel it is, but won't say now." What a shocked look came over Mickey's face! Bug-eyed like the night he dashed by me. They left! I looked at all the police coming toward him, questioning him more. The customers hurried out, and I remained alone. Oh, dear! Then another cop walked in.

He got out his pad to confirm it, I supposed, but I was not well all of a sudden. I gave my name and address, then mumbled, "I don't feel well and want to sit down. I was scared, I didn't trust him!" Whew! Finally he walked out.

I phoned Charles to tell him what happened. "And I'm just shaking, and going to cry. No, I can't go home and close the store, because Brad is coming in for an ad this week. I will be all right later, I think. I can't realize he's caught yet. My mind hasn't told my body to quit being afraid."

I had mixed feelings about sending a *customer* to jail, but that was where he belonged. So glad no one was there to shop; I liked to rest awhile. The phone rang and Detective Parks asked how I was. "I'm okay now. Yes, it's him."

I just sat there rehashing and tried to call Angela, no luck. The phone again; it was Lisa. I said, "The detective wants to question Angela and me, but I can't reach her. I'm feeling better, but I can't relax. Lisa, he's caught and *we did it!* What if your phone had been busy? God knew I was numb. Okay, I'll have Brad call you when he comes. I don't want any more young guys to enter that door today! Bye."

I spoke too soon. One did, with his arms full of large framed pictures, or posters. He came to me at the counter and I hesitated. What a handsome, mannerly young man he was. He asked, "May I show you some pictures I'm selling to work my way through school? They're photos by the head photographer of National Geographic."

I was not really interested, all things considered, but was willing to look. He didn't know of my raw feelings, how vulnerable I was. The prints were very beautiful. "May I see that sunset over the lake again, please?" I asked the price and added, "I'll take that one. It's my favorite subject. I need that in my family room."

I knew I wouldn't forget that day, or him-a nice, polite man, I guessed. We chatted about his home town across the state, since I used to live there. I was glad he came and took my mind off Mickey, and he had a little less to carry. Strange, he had the same first name.

Brad came in finally for an ad order, and I related what happened over tea and cookies. That pesky phone again! I heard the words, "I issued a warrant for Mickey's arrest, a subpoena for you and Angela, and the prosecutor is planning a hearing. You will be informed when," Detective Parks announced. What a relief!

Imagine Mickey stupid enough to show his face again. But when he was never picked up, though in December we identified him, he probably figured the danger was past. I wouldn't remember him and he could case us before we closed, or rob us again today. Lisa told me a surprising fact, that the police dispatch operator delayed her plea for help to my store, though she informed the operator the thief returned who had robbed it. She asked for Lisa's name and address repeatedly, and finally Lisa became angry. This gave Mickey time by the window before I came to ring up the shorts his buddy saw earlier.

Brad left me then; I had famous last words, "They said he wouldn't come back; God sent him back." When I told Angela everything, we co-conspirators in crime-solving laughed together. Then I wondered, "Do you think he might have come in to merely talk and I jumped the gun, getting him arrested? Jail is a terrible place and I'd hate to ruin him there."

She practically shouted, "No way!"

"I'll take your experienced judgment over mine. The enemy confronted became the enemy confounded. Whoopee!"

Testifying in Court

This was the memorable day we'd been waiting for–the hearing. Lisa was to mind the store, she and her little boy to keep her company. Brad planned to have lunch with them. And off Angela and I went with fear and palpitations.

"We'll tell you everything, Lisa, you know that."

We heroines returned to her–after we stopped for lunch, which made sense. If they could eat, things couldn't be too bad, so she took a bet with Brad there would be a trial. I began, "The case was cut and dried. The prosecutor and Detective Parks met us in the hall of district court and discussed my case. They said, 'Mickey denied he robbed you and couldn't remember where he was that night–real cool, too. He had said to the policeman who met him outside your door that he knew he should have had his hair cut!'

"That policeman was quickly summoned to witness for me. When Mickey arrived with his attendant and court appointed female lawyer, his eyes were as big as quarters, his manner aloof, even defiant. I wondered if that was why he wore the clothes he bought from my store.

"The policeman who swore me in was a customer, in fact he had bought a down jacket a couple of weeks before. I hated repeating my name and address for the court stenographer, fearing Mickey's friends were in the courtroom. A pretty girl with long, dark hair watched me while I testified to the events of the robbery.

"The prosecutor asked me to relate all that happened. What time? Could I see his face? Was I alone? What did he have on? I told him I loosened my wrists the first time he tied me, but I didn't reach the back door as I planned. What did he take? Who called the police? And my voice didn't weaken, as it does when I'm nervous. Mickey glowered, but some in court glared at him, too.

"Once he scribbled notes to his lawyer. Then the prosecutor asked me to describe what happened when he came the second time. Did I recognize him? Who called the police? Is he in the room? Where? And I was *sure.*

"His lawyer checked her notes, inquiring, 'Did you see his face? How far away was he from you?'

"'Three feet,' I answered.

"'His nose round, small, large?'

"'No, average.' I remembered.

"'Color of eyes? Lips thin or full?'

"'They were pulled tight,' I added.

"'The reason why I called Lisa, not the police? Were you not sure it was him?'

"'His walk, face, and body language were enough, but I wanted to observe a while to be sure of my sureness. He wasn't robbing me, so I wondered what he came for.'

"'Next the policeman who arrested him testified. The judge said, 'Step down.'

"'Afterward, Detective Parks said, 'We're doing fine. The judge will arraign next week.' We don't have to go. That's the story, Lisa."

"See, Mom, I knew we had a case."

"I'm not finished. The man in the parked car behind my store the night of the robbery was present and praised my testimony. With the fingerprints and all this, we're in good shape. The pretty girl telephoned someone afterward.

"At lunch Angela and I discussed Mickey and wished he would somehow while in jail let God change his life goals. We don't hate him. I wish I could influence the judge at a trial if he's found guilty to sentence a work penalty. Those eyes haunt me, I admit. He was in jail all this time, but I thought he might have been out on bond; one never knows. So the case rests for us. I suppose the trial is weeks away. I'm sure going to court is not my bag; I wish he'd plead guilty and eliminate a trial. That's worse than today, isn't it, Angela? And it costs an arm and a leg for the taxpayers."

"He's too cool to admit he's guilty, especially if he's already got a police record. What a day!" Angela walked to the back room for a while. Lisa collected her young one and belongings to head for home and rest.

Harassed and Encouraged

Those days in February, the month of my fifty-eighth birthday, certainly intimidated me. Where were the simple ways and rules of early school days? Wash your hands before you eat. Warm cookies and cold milk are good for you. Live a balanced life: learn some, think, draw, paint, sing, play, and work every day. Take a nap every afternoon. Think of what a better world it would be if we all, the whole world, lay down with our blankets for a nap.

But no, I had to face–as the new woman–the newer world. The hearing was just the beginning of challenges. One Monday afternoon when I arrived, someone waited for me. I wasn't ready for customers, as I was late and hardly cared. He was another crummy looking young guy. But I opened the door after stashing the money back under the counter–no time to fill the register. I asked him, "Is there anything special you need?"

"No, I want to look at the jackets." What else? And he seemed to know right where they were. Never saw him before either; I merely pointed to the rack now, telling him to help himself. He didn't try any on; like the last one, none buy. He fit the pattern to a "t."

I picked up the phone to call again. Oh, I heard a busy buzz, so my fake conversation could only set him thinking. It did, the turkey left. He gave me a cold stare. Was he part of a stolen goods ring, planning to harass us while liquidating? I heard a rumor that Mickey hired a lawyer, so there would be a trial or a plea bargain.

He had a crime pattern. Angela thought he could be sentenced to prison if he lost.

"So he planned to fight it? What a heel! He surely fooled us that first time he came to buy clothes. I thought we might be friends, but he was a hood," I surmised.

Later a struggling businessman drew out my empathy. He economically operated a photography shop in his house. I liked his black hair, with a touch of gray and dark eyes. Sounded like a creative perfectionist, trying new methods and cost cutting in time and money for his customers–not bad. He was better than the average man coming in, and when I hinted my store might be rented for other businesses or hobby and craft displays, he perked up. "I checked the mall, which is too steep, but I need the flow of customers downtown offers. You made my day! My wife works, so I can work at home, but my income is poor. She does my bookkeeping for me." Sounded familiar. We exchanged cards. With another year's lease, we had to be open to alternatives to utilize it, and look–the first word we learned in the Dick and Jane beginning reader, days of simple ways and rules.

Patience

I was not known for my patience–my handwriting analyst claimed I liked to roll along, move on to other heights, endeavors, whatever. This pertained to my customers and their actions, too. Now some were moseying around everything, trying on all we had in three sizes of pants. One girl broke the zipper of the smaller jeans and then they mentioned, "Nothing appeals to us, we might be back."

But I inwardly muttered, I hope not; after all that I'm beat. I tried to help them throughout the store. Next, I noticed a little man who had been in three times and bought nothing.

"How much off for this jacket?" he asked. Angela answered him.

"How much are you asking for the sweater?" she answered again. "Will you be marking it down more?"

"No!" What was the bird up to?

"What about this blazer?" he asked three times. I could see Angela was seething.

He informed her, "I'm not cheap." He was a short, bearded man who reminded me of some suppliers I had. I dealt with them a lot and considered them very helpful to me with buying advice and pricing. By making her quote the prices over and over, he hoped to drive them lower, a trick she was on to. I wondered why she didn't just walk away. She did, she was so disgusted and tired of the tightwad.

Well, how about that? He carried three items to the counter to buy; her strategy worked? No dummy, that Angela. He was like a vulture at the feast and didn't know it.

Little men–I wondered if they were related sometimes. They fit a pattern, it seemed–the careful consumer, but could be aggressive. One arrived with glasses, graying hair, fingering all the men's wear while he stated, "I have closets full, I really don't need anymore, but I like a deal when I can get one. I'm retired," he told me. "I'll be back with a friend. You open tonight?"

"Yes, until eight o'clock."

Wonder of wonders, he came back with a lady who looked considerably younger and rather passive. Maybe he'd taken her under his wing; that was nice of him. They were very particular, and inspected my cheapest salesmen's samples. Though he chose some not her style, she seemed grateful anyway. He was lousy at matching colors, and tops with skirts. I heard him say, as I offered assistance, "No, I've made my bundle, want to spend some on her."

Well, I didn't complain. I was so happy to sell those older items. They were below cost and good quality. When they came to me to pay, he asked the girl, "Does that take care of it now?"

"I'm not sure; I didn't get a white blouse yet and I like this one." She held up a new style, white, long-sleeved with lace inserts down the front.

Noting the price was higher than anything in the pile, he hesitated, then said, "Well, okay." I rang up a nice sale for a Friday night. Charles watched in the wings, as nothing else happened to break his boredom. He had replaced all the dead florescent tubes by then.

Heading toward the door, our generous friend noticed the calfskin mitts and gloves in the front wagon. "I could use a small. The price of your gloves here is too high," he noted in passing. "This time of year we mark down 20 percent off the retail price on the ticket," I explained. But he coyly smiled, "Oh, I don't need them, because I'm always losing one or the other."

Really now, we knew the price wasn't low enough; that's how he made his bundle, no doubt.

One never knew what to expect from a barter system customer. And we didn't when we purchased their services and goods either, a new concept. One such customer had been in before, telling me he drove from another town as there were no other clothing stores on the system. So we traded. "He made a haul the last time," I told Angela, "blazers, sweaters, cords, jeans, thermal underwear."

"He sure did; didn't Lisa alter the lengths of many pants because he's not tall?" I agreed.

He said, "I'm spending a fortune again today. I'll call friends about your boot sale—four dollars can't be beat." Those boots had been a steal for months, but he just discovered it. I saw his interest in a navy down jacket. Did I hear right?

"I'd take this if you'd lower the price five dollars," he offered. "No, they're down to cost." Liquidating didn't mean giving it away.

"Hold it for a day," he ordered.

He hustled in on Saturday with a friend, likely for the jacket. I was on the phone and Angela had a customer. He breezed back to me to take it *now*, very impatient, but I decided he must learn to wait his turn. I entailed a 10 percent handling fee, for which I charged, but gave quality buys for units. He didn't want the jacket in a bag-hurry, hurry. Angela wasn't impressed, I could tell.

There came a sad day that took more than my patience-my energy began to seep away with it. I related the story at work. "Angela, did you hear the latest? Charles broke his right wrist yesterday when he fell at the house of Sally, one of our girls, helping the family move in."

"You've got to be kidding."

"That's why I need you on Monday, since I must drive him to the doctor. My new title is caregiver."

"Really? Is it a bad break? How did he do it?" She looked sympathetic.

"Slipped backwards on ice. He can't drive or write so he won't work this week. I must do the store books now, too. What timing! He won't be able to move boxes or racks here for weeks. What'll I do?" I complained.

"I'll bet the other men in your family will do anything you ask. Don't worry. Have patience and take a potent vitamin. He's no help anywhere now. That's a bummer, if I ever heard of one." Angela put her arm across my shoulders and squeezed.

Another day, another customer! "Believe me, Angela, this lady, so gentle looking, sure drives a hard bargain. She looks for flaws, broken zippers, and compares each item to get markdowns. Her daughter usually comes with her, though only after school. I'm a good judge of character, first glance and all. She's unique," I commented quietly.

She agreed. "Oh, I remember her. I spent scads of time with her one Saturday and wondered about her methods. She left to price shop in other stores, came back, and bought one item. Then she compared across the street, returned, and said, 'You have the cheapest of several stores we went to all afternoon.'"

I concurred, "Glad she was finally convinced. We could have told her that, saved her gas and time, right? Notice now that we're closing, she's here every week to check the latest markdowns and buys more. Even asks why some are different than others. She must know we buy at varied prices; keeps us hopping just to answer her. Some items don't qualify so she tries to figure how to make them do so. Isn't that irritating?"

"Um hum. One time she kept me overtime while she fed clothes to her girl in the fitting room. Last time, she bought more pants and a sweater and used the girl's bus money, she was so anxious to get the last big deal. She sweetly gave us her pennies, 'because we gave her so many good buys,' she said. 'I wish you well as I won't see you again. We'll miss your store,' and smiled at me."

"That figures. She made over her wardrobe very cheaply. Why do people think *such prices* would *remain* if *we* did? How do we pay bills? Is profit a dirty word? She's great, just great!" I was exasperated, obviously.

"That's merely trading dollars on your donated time, right? Retail!"

"We can't win for losing, Angela. And we're not the only ones with straining patience. Our neighbor from the mall, Gwen, visited us here a couple of times and hasn't found a job for over a year. I went to her yard sale, as she was hurting when she lost unemployment benefits. Now on subsistence pay only.

"Last week, she wanted answers to questions for a resume project. Seems an agency for an ethnic group offered her this to find a job. She's so happy to know help is available. The questions were the same an applicant asked me last fall."

"Oh, like what?" Angela wondered.

"Let me get another cup of coffee," I said. "Well, what do you look for in a salesperson?" I continued. "What character traits are helpful? I answered that I looked for a pleasant person, who is honest, retail–experienced if possible with basic math ability–one who wants to learn new job aspects. I preferred someone with no race bias, ambitious, and willing to do some light maintenance. Retail skills include taking inventory, display-ing, checking merchandise, and marking it according to codes. Of course, I'm spoiled with my capable Angela, and Lisa always does my inventory quickly and efficiently." Angela beamed.

"Gwen told me about a new gift store in her old spot, so I shopped there. She feels competition from like stores in the mall will be rough. There are new black holes on that floor, and the store whose racks we used is iffy. Too bad."

"That's par for retail, you know," Angela smirked.

"But what would we do without it? It's indispensable, popular worldwide, challenging—need I say more?" And tries my patience often to the nth *degree*, I muttered silently.

Fearful

It dawned on me, finally, that a numbing was taking place in me as I felt my business fail. I feared danger, detested my suspicions and silent harass-ment from the drug world. Also I sensed drugs were thicker than blood or water in the veins of addicts or users.

One day I thought, I do believe Mickey kindly referred another friend, from his gang maybe, to case the jackets. A tall man with the same shifty, unkempt look, about his age. His black hair showed below his hood, but he didn't loiter as long as the others did. I noted the color jacket he had on. It looked as shabby as others had worn, a light gold quilted. He inspected the calfskin mitts. I walked toward him.

"You've good prices on your jackets. What time do you close?" he asked. I quoted my closing time. "I'll be back for some!" he commented.

He left, but I worried muttering, "Why don't those characters buy them now, and quit coming, saying they'll be back? At closing *again*? Working alone is scary when these guys might be harassing me. Angela or Lisa ought to be here at the end today."

I answered the phone, Angela's call. I complained to her about it. Then Brad came and got an earful. "I'm suspicious of that man. If he's coming for something, how do you figure it? Rob me? Or buy them? With other guys, too?

Brad offered, "I'll try to stop by about four-thirty to check and stay if I can arrange it." What a relief!

"Good! Angela said she'd be over, too, and prepare a plan with me. What a way to go! Now we're using our noggins. How much of this uncertainty can we take around here?" Brad agreed.

My scheme? We should be scattered in the store with Angela near the back to call police, if necessary. With Brad in sight, I won't feel vulnerable. Angela arrived, suggesting a game plan, too. She would fake a police call, taking the cord to the back room with the door chain caught. I didn't want all three of us ordered to the floor with jackets stolen before our very eyes. Then she'd run out the back door, if necessary. I removed excess money from the register. It was 4:45 and we were ready. I'm glad we didn't stay open till 5:30 anymore, the suspense would kill me.

Angela chatted, "This is exciting, just like big time, ready for the robbery with our stake out. Is someone watching from outside to see if we're alone, maybe?"

"Could be, and with all this help, he won't dare try anything. I want to be kind and fair to everybody, and not suspect unless given a reason to. It's like the devil's out to change me! I don't like myself this way. It's hard to love people if your defenses are up all day long. You could be anyone's enemy and not know it, and they're stronger than you. It's mind boggling."

"Well, either he didn't intend to do it, or he came back and saw us all, because at five o'clock I lock the door for the day. But how's that saying go? An ounce of prevention is worth a pound of cure. Who wants that act to prove you are ready? Curtain time." What price, fear and suspicion!

Frustrated

Way back, in show and tell, we saw goldfish, hamsters, white mice, and little seeds in cups...and they all died. In frustration we wondered why. And so it goes.

"Angela, I suspect we are going to meet our busy neighbor. He spied our clearance sale banner. From rumors I heard, he's in a health and exercise business. He told me, 'It's aerobics, and I have apartments upstairs where I'll live when the furnace is replaced.'"

He greeted us and chatted till he got to the point. "I heard about your robbery; I'm surprised the thief came back. He did, really? Sure glad he's in jail. I don't want the likes of him in my building. He obviously strikes twice in the same spot, like lightning." I agreed.

"I had an experience once, a dilly. I worked at a place on the edge of town when in high school-two stores were together, men's and women's. One day, the manager of the women's came, white and scared, into ours, toward us guys chatting and laughing. She had been robbed at gun point by a big guy who took some of her furs. I saw him dash out, so I followed in my car to get his license number, but the plate was bent. The thief pointed his gun through the car window at me! I left!"

"How awful! Guns scare me. What happened next?"

"I saw him again at a gas station and read the license number that time. I gave it to the police, who took me to the address to identify him. We saw the car in front, but the police wouldn't go in for him. Feared false arrest charges, maybe? Or part of an underground ring, and he knew the furs were peddled by then? I'll never know. My boss at that store had his tale of woe, too. When he left a customer downstairs to wait while going up for his layaway, the man stole some of his leather coats. He was gone when he came down. He later saw the crook in the mall wearing one of his coats but could do nothing about it. That's the law for retail today." Then he left us, more frustrated.

I pondered, "So how can we gals win? Catch 'em going out the store with the goods, but women are helpless against a big man. It's a bad scene, wears me down. I travel miles to get here on slippery roads, even in the dark since time changed, and for what? We both burn the midnight oil to balance the books, pay bills, file tax returns, discuss orders, sales, decisions–what a life!"

But I told Angela, "I like the work basically, the buying trips, and the friends we've made. I learned a lot, too, and can say that again. Too much about the crummy aspects. Not worth dying for either."

Breaking Down

It was a lovely day in March, but I came in very late and felt and looked exhausted-not as feisty as I used to be. Once I told Angela, "I feel like I've a broken rudder. The fun is gone since I can't trust people anymore."

I should have stayed in bed. I cashed the register, wishing no one appeared to be suspected. A bright day is good for all sorts of things, except working, really.

Lisa and Kim entered alone! "What are you up to?"

Lisa answered, "I've some skirts and pants I shortened for you, Mom. A couple of customers wanted them by Saturday. We're on our way to Midtown for a shopping spree."

"I'm green with envy. I'd go with you; I can't endure this today. My brain stopped, I'm numb, ready for the loony bin, I think," I moaned.

"You alone today?"

"No, Angela is coming in an hour."

"Well, call her to come earlier and go with us. Don't you dare stay here," Kim ordered. I called her; she would.

"We'll make two stops before meeting you outside of town, Mom. Okay? At eleven o'clock, see you."

I saw Angela coming, and right behind her was the weirdo in pigtails. I wondered, Does he braid his own? I wouldn't leave till he was gone. No one should be alone with him, if it could be helped.

He stalled something awful in the back at the men's blazers. Maybe he had no place to go but wander in and out of stores. My girls would have to wait awhile, thanks to him. He told Angela his father died in Indiana and he needed a blazer for his funeral. He fingered every one. She said, "That's too bad. Do you want to try them on? Do you plan to get one today?"

"No, I'll have to come back later, I don't have the money." He poked along–a basket case! Finally, he quit the chitchat with Angela.

I told her, "I couldn't leave you alone with him; he's the one I had Lisa call the police for. If I had to face him alone in my condition, I'd have bawled in his face, I'm so nervous."

"Well, get out of here and have a fun day with your girls." Angela shooed me out the door, pronto. She did not expect him back.

Just then a nice boy who sold Grit Magazine walked in. She knew him over a period of time, as they chatted, and she bought because she liked him, though his paper appealed to her also.

She told me later, "I hear he's won some boy scout medals and is happy to tell me about it. He lives with his proud dad–broken home, I guess. I sure will miss him. And Tom, our mailman, who's a good friend, since he knows us from the mall. Many wonderful people come here, including Detective Park's mother. I knew her from my last job."

These were the sorrows that broke our spirits, too, as I remembered Angela has a loving character.

Pawn Shop?

I suppose one could think his education incomplete if he never entered a pawn shop. I never found the need nor had a desire, so my mind ignored the subject, until one day while we were liquidating all stock.

"We're really popular today, aren't we, Angela? It's exhilarating. Last week was the pits, boring, you name it. Don't you like to watch the men? But they avoid us like we're diseased now. I see one coming who doesn't palpitate my pulse, though he was not drab when younger, I suspect. Note the tall, dark-haired one with the wrinkled face and slight shuffle."

I left her, to talk to him by the counter and cash register. He had a brown paper bag in his hand. I heard him say something quietly. "What do you want?" I asked.

"Do you buy things here? Things to sell?"

"Nothing now. I sell only clothes and I'm going out of business."

But he didn't seem to understand. He held out a small radio from his bag and begged. "I want to sell my radio. Please give me something for it." Poor guy, looked like he'd hit rock bottom, hard luck. Either that or he drank too much.

"I can't buy anything. I'm going out of business, I'm emptying my store."

And he muttered, "I know what you mean. I'm empty, too. Won't you buy this? I'm out of a job." He didn't look me in the eye and didn't give up. He could have used a bath, among other things.

I told him, "I feel for you. Maybe you need a pawn shop, but I don't know of any near here. I guess you need God's help, too, don't you?" He mumbled something in a slurred voice and shuffled out the door, clutching his little bag. Poor man.

"Angela, that reminds me of a pretty teenage girl who dashed in once with a scarf for me to buy. She must have some money now for who knows what. We've had all types of people here, makes retail interesting, right?"

"That isn't all it does, by a long shot. I won't go into details," she laughed.

"Want to hear a choice bit of news, Angela? It will go down in the history books of the establishment. Are you superstitious? Last week, on Friday the 13th, we made the most sales of any day since our existence, way over one thousand dollars. I'm preserving the tape for posterity!"

"I don't know how to read that momentous omen, really."

"Maybe I could run out my lease with a pawn shop, the thought just passed through my mind."

"No, you don't need their typical clientele. But it does feel good to be so busy, the cash register pings all the time."

Loyalty and Replacement

Some customers really tried to keep me in business, deliberately or not, I figured. I noticed a lady with glasses and a sweet smile, who was a shy and loyal customer for me at both stores. She was big on coats and bought some from us. Lisa did an alterations job that beat the average–inner lining, too. One day the woman checked to see if we received any new coats for the winter. I had found no salesmen's samples in attractive styles that year, so she was disappointed.

"I'm surprised you're still here. Guess you'll stay till you sell most of the clothes, won't you?"

"Yes, that makes sense to me. Our lease goes on even after we close."

Angela came up to me, commenting, "You can't see it from here, but the way mannequin Alexandra is leaning, one leg seems to protrude so that she looks pregnant. Depends on your angle, of course, and if not brought to your attention, no one will notice."

"Oh, well, fault of the manufacturer, I suppose. Do you like the bright outfit she's modeling? Perfect with her hair. By the way, that lady browsing found a coat in Midtown, as our store offers slim pickings now. I'm glad for her. She tried on a pair of cranberry pants like mine and a white top, though not her size." I turned to the customer, "Now that velour housecoat looks good on you. I have one like it from my daughter for Christmas. It feels comfortable and it washed beautifully. I'll think of you when I wear mine. How about that?"

Then my friend said, "I wish you well, whatever you do. What do you plan to do?"

"I have no specific plans but I must put something here if we don't sublease it. Nothing competing with mall business, you know."

"Well, I know of a bakery in my town, makes delicious turnovers and Danish rolls that might consider a branch store downtown here."

I suggested, "I'll call them. I had a business like that in mind. Some of the neighbors proposed it."

I told Angela later, "Sometimes it's who you know, not what you know. That would be great if I found one others want."

I called that bakery in the afternoon. "It seemed like the manager was interested. He had been searching in the mall, but rents were too high, so he liked my ideas," I revealed to Angela. "And he'll check my place soon. Also Tom, the mailman, would love coffee with his rolls, and is on our side. I called Lisa; she was so excited, she ended, 'Say a prayer, he's the one for us.'"

To anyone who told me I would have to replace my own business, I'd say, "You're daft!"

Being Deceived

You'd think I was adept at spotting crooks by then, but perpetual vigilance was not my forte, nor would it ever be.

I had a super day! Such remarkable people dropped in, too. They were crazy about the big sale those days, and with markdowns like mine, they should be. I felt successful, if you could call it that, when practically giving it all away. Then I looked at scarecrow Elsie when all had left and realized I'd never changed her old checked sweater for two years, and her hair was all gone. She wore that same old straw beach hat with the pompom missing, and her hands had lost their mitts. She looked forlorn.

Once I asked Charles, "Let me offer one of the scarecrows to the Montessori School behind the store, okay?" He agreed it was a good idea, whatever kind of school that was. "I dunno," I said dimly.

Reality hit me then. Here entered a big, smiling woolly-haired man with shades on-and no sun. "I didn't plan to come in, but thought better of it." He gave bills to me at the cash register and asked, "May I have a twenty dollar bill for these? They didn't have any next door. Do you need any help to work here? My wife needs a job. We're from the South."

I gave him twenty dollars from the till while answering, "I'm closing so I don't intend to hire anyone."

He stared at the counter and me, "You gave me a one dollar bill, see?"

That dirty dog! That's all I need to top my good day! Naturally, I denied it. "No, I did not. I know I gave you a twenty dollar bill. What do you mean?"

I listened to him lie, "Look, you can search my pockets! I work, too, and I would not take your money. See my empty pockets?"

"No, I won't search you! But I know how many twenty dollar bills I had, and *yours* is one of them. I suppose it's your word against mine, isn't it?" He was a big man and I would *never* win this one, if I refused. Getting flustered, I started to say, "Here, take these back," but then I didn't let him, knowing I'd be out more. I couldn't give in, but I knew he wouldn't either. I hoped he had no gun to pull on me; his smile was deceiving.

"Here, see these empty pockets? I have only this one dollar bill you put here on the counter." I decided, I won't be stupid enough to touch him. He'd slipped it up his sleeve, and I knew it, too. What a bother! Someone, come in that door! No use banging my head against a stone wall.

"Oh, here then, I know what I gave you," I exploded. "It's people like you that are driving me out of business!" I threw him another twenty dollars and put the one dollar in the till, so angry I could spit. He walked jauntily and opened the door. *What a cheater!*

I called Lisa, ready to cry. Why do people do this to me? Lisa comforted me as best she could. I agreed, "I know I can't change anything now, but I work for *nothing* and give in to these creeps of society. It hurts! He sure took the shine off my day. Why does *anyone* want a retail business?"

She reassured me, "Well, the end's in sight for you, though I know each day drags on. Till the end of March, or everything's liquidated. You won't have to force yourself to say good-bye, remember."

"True. I pity those who have to make a living this way. I hope they keep a stiff upper lip and a sense of humor. Your dad is worn down from the bookwork this place gives him; he's good and fast, but he's lost his zip, too."

So much for slippery prevaricators in retail!

Insulted

When a certain customer came in, I had to remind myself, This is *my* store, I don't have to be here–I don't *need* the money.

Deah, deah, get a peek at this la-de-da gal! She shopped here before? She has a familiar ring somehow. But she has on a short blonde wig; there are changes, along with her expensive duds and furs. That makeup is a bit heavy. I am being catty, but I recall something snobbish she said the last time she was in. Oh, yes, ma'am. It was for sale items to wear "around the house" and to inquire about the robbery, which we didn't discuss with her. Angela knows her from her old job, and found her to be a pain-and that's something for unbiased Angela.

Then I remembered...she had come in two weeks before and asked for Angela. "I see you're closing? Suppose your robbery caused that? Hmm, not much left, is there? Nothing I can use." Obviously she was checking.

"I think you have some mens' blazers my husband and son could bum around in, so how much?"

I told her, "Ten dollars and 30 percent off."

She admitted, "They can't go wrong for that, to wear as we travel." She used the phone to call her husband. "He works at Dotel Company and can drop right over to try them on, since both take the same size."

I thought, *That's mighty big of her.* Guess we want to move those couple blazers, but does she have to put down our better items? I reminded her, "There are no exchanges now, so he must try them on." I thought I heard Angela come in the back door from the Snack Shack with her coffee. She peeked, saw madam, then motioned to me to keep quiet that she was back. She wouldn't take over, as I wanted her to. Did I blame her? Sounded like Madam had her husband on the line.

"Dear, can you come see me at this little store going out of business? It has some junk you might be able to use, some blazers to run around in."

I seethed inside, *That's vulgar! What a cad!*

Then she pumped me a bit. "What are you going to do now? What is Angela going to do?"

I supposed I had to answer, though I didn't know why; none of her business, really. I hinted, "We *may* sublease to a bakery or flower shop."

A tall, gangling, ordinary looking man with glasses arrived–her man. I showed him the jackets and such condescending gestures I never did see as he glanced at them. He laughed at the short sleeves, but they were true to size; his arms were long. I offered my seamstress services to lengthen them.

He decided, "No, it's too short in the back, too."

Madam had found another buy for him. "Here's some vinyl raincoats for three dollars; could you use any?"

After trying on a medium, he growled, 'No!"

She continued, "*Your* jacket is just as short as this tan with a denim look. We could have Jen make the sleeves longer for Ted, you know." I couldn't believe those people. He agreed, pompously.

"What are your fees? Can you do better than two dollars?"

I was so proud of my patience. "Look at my list by the fitting rooms. I don't remember. I doubt that!"

He hurried back to see the six dollar fee, and told Madam. She was against it. "Not for a seven dollar jacket." And he agreed. (Really–that was thirty-five dollars originally.)

"That's fine, I'll take it to your seamstress. She works for Dades. Cut off the tags, dear. I don't want her to see where we got it."

Unbelievable! He thinks he's God's gift to man, I could tell. Then the power company meter reader arrived. He walked toward the back door, then into the front again. Seemed uncertain of what he wanted. He came in and asked to leave by the back door, if I would lock the door after him. Strange! Just couldn't make up his mind? Surprise!

Our tall drink-of-water offered, "I'll lock up after him for you."

Then I was nervous, "No, Angela can do it instead." I was sure she didn't want him back there to snoop around; he had no business back there! But he did it anyway. He'd see Angela, and she wouldn't like that. Nothing happened, however.

Angela peeked out. "What a gutsy guy! Have they left?"

"Yes, finally. Nuts! He forgot his old topcoat." I called out the door for him.

Madam yelled and laughed, "You could keep that and sell it with *your* old things."

"What brass! She's left with her big, quivering *ego!*"

Angela grinned, "Be thankful for small favors; we'll never see them again."

Eliminated and Liquidated

In a way, those two thoughts seem synonymous; harsh reality, I suppose.

"Angela, did you know we're not invited to the last style show in the mall, though our next door neighbors will have booths? Of course, they know we're liquidating–besides, we have no spring merchandise. The new styles are gross-loose, wrinkled, and shapeless, the flapper era waist length and hems below the calf," I described, after viewing Chicago's Michigan Avenue shops that week. I was glad I didn't have to promote them.

"This show will be different." I quoted from the newspaper, "The fashions will be paired with music and move to the narration of a disc jockey from a radio station...the models will not walk solo down the runway that doubles as a dock, but will move in groups of two, three, and five-building from the casual to the dressy, as the show progresses, using merchandise from sixteen downtown stores. It makes the show go faster and is much more interesting; there will be men and women modeling."

"Incidentally, Angela," I continued, "men's underwear styles wouldn't be for us either." I read on, "The shorts will be brief; scant, abbreviated drawers one rip away from the indecent exposure. For Valentine's Day, drawers everywhere are more open in their appeal to the beat man, blowzy boxers with hearts and flowers suffering in outrageous swings of Cupid's arrow; or the five dollar red bikini brief, or the King of Hearts, showing a king of hearts, playing card variety." I saw some displayed then.

"Isn't it sad, it's the end of an era for us; we're just slipping away into the dark night. It gets me right here. Our style shows had pizzazz, remember?"

"What a shame; my glory is waning, too," Angela quipped.

Sometimes I felt despair, not knowing what triggered it. I asked her, "Why am I a *success* only if I make *money*? If I helped some people to have a better life with my store, am I a *success*? I *chose* to have a *full* chance at retail, though I admit my *best* ways were not enough to win."

"You did fine," she reassured me.

"Are my reactions, feeling defeated and wasted, natural? I know the excuses or reasons are real, but I try not to think of my future if things get murky. I'm ready for the freedom and time to relax, though, so I am not devastated." We slowly sipped our tea, thinking and mulling over our lot.

"Not to change the subject, but those teachers from the Montessori School like to shop here on their lunch hour. They're young mothers who need culottes, wrap skirts, and pants for floor work with the kids. They love our bargains, too."

"I know; I offered to give the school a scarecrow for the children if the teachers thought they could use it. They liked the idea. We're giving Cecil," I informed her.

In fantasy, I supposed that Alexandra said to crow Elsie, "That would please Cecil, wouldn't it? I'm so sorry he never fell for me."

"Oh, don't take his slights seriously. He needs a purpose in life, you know. He's been stuck in the back room, we never heard from him. Slept all the time, or mumbled under his breath about the dark hole he was in."

"Oh, Elsie, a maintenance man came for him at the front door with his car. He said, 'Nuts! I can't fit him in it after all. I'll carry him out the back door through the parking lot."

"Bye, Cecil! There he goes, slung over his shoulder; Cecil's hat and arms are bobbing high over the man's head. He looks so funny. He is now 'liquidated,' Alexandra. I'd weep if I could…"

"Elsie, here comes some mothers from the school. He's been there a while now."

"Yes, I heard one of them tell Angela that Cecil scared her every time she looked up. She thought a man was staring at her. Naturally, they moved him to another spot, and agreed they'll miss us, too. Isn't that nice of them?"

"You're all heart, Elsie. I could almost cry, but it would smudge my finish, wouldn't it? I will control myself."

I found gradual changes bearable and, when taken one at a time, rather interesting. Likely it was because I had so little to do now and could analyze them more. A great change in my life would soon begin: no business.

Sharing the Remnants

The word was out: down to the remnants; going fast.

"Oh, oh, Angela, batten down the hatches! Here come some of my little people, raring to go. They're with their moms but you know who has to protect the property, what's left of it."

"Sure do!" Angela greeted them lovingly as usual. You'd think they were hers, too.

"I told the family to check for the last time what they want before their sizes and choices are gone. They've been my regular customers because we had such good buys and styles for over two years. I've set aside items for their birthdays and next Christmas for that reason. The merchandise is really low now, even those down jackets—one men's left and five women's. Imagine that! Never thought I'd *outlive* that *popular* item. There's a pretty, rust-colored coat with fur collar for Kim's Lori, a bit large but next year she can wear it nicely. And some need our toddlers' snowsuits, not expensive when below cost."

Lisa wanted some skirt and coat hangers for her seamstress business. The decorations were up for grabs. Kim wanted a fitting room mirror, too, and the cedar chest in the window. As customers asked to buy wagons and fixtures, we were slowly finding places for everything. The cash register was advertised at a good price.

Angela and I chose coats some time back, each getting all-weather coats and hooded winter coats, blouses, sweaters, blazers to match pants and skirts we fit into. We had more fun consulting each other. Charles said, "Take whatever you want, as the remainder goes to charities—tax deductible."

I commented to her, "When we had family parties, all arrived in my latest garb, so this business has been important to my clan. Even the grandchildren were proud and greeted me, 'Look what I have on today, Grandma!' All wardrobes got bigger."

We watched the commotion with pleasure. "Angela, I haven't heard whether or not that man who plans a deli in here resolved his problems with the health department. He can't afford all their changes and outfit the store accordingly to his early plans: small tables and chairs for the customers eating sandwiches and sampling his international coffees and teas. He'd sell quality candy and treats. But he must fix a rest room for the handicapped, and install long sinks in the back room with boiling water. At the last check, he was afraid the deal was off. Both he and I imagined great possibilities for the people who work around here. I also contacted other florists and bakeries for this place, but no luck."

"That's too bad for everybody around, really. I'm sorry." Angela had told the mailman our plans and hopes.

"I heard Lori tell Kim she'd like to take crow Elsie to their farm since she helped make her. A pro golf shop owner hinted about Alexandra but I wondered if he were serious. A tailor desired her just for her torso, so I did not commit her. He also needed my work tables, fitting rooms with curtains, storage shelves, and odd items. I might not be around much longer!

I sold many supplies and plus size clothes to a pretty girl managing a new store in Lawton. Alexandra would put some pizzazz in her window if she wished to have her."

A screaming Julio entered her window. His sister chased him through the store while Kim tried on pants. Oops, he fell, so Grandma scooped him up and out. Had to save her, as her future elsewhere was at stake.

"Well, there they all go for today, Angela. I must repair the damage-those scattered free hangers under the wagon and the books with crayons strewn around. I don't mind, though, I suppose I can take anything about now, huh? The *end* is in sight, though I'm tired."

"Naturally. I'll work only on your day off and Saturdays now and stay till the store closes. I have not applied for another job anywhere yet. I've had some offers, but not full time."

"I appreciate that. We're not very busy anymore, so phone or do whatever you like. I feel we're very good friends after all we've been through together. Let's keep in touch. I wonder if Charles dislikes telling his friends I didn't succeed."

"I don't think so because the store served its purpose while needed and the family benefited. One is not a failure if one sincerely tries. It was better before all those changes came, so....." Angela doodled on a pad.

"I know. I had to roll with the punches, that's all. It improved our marriage, too. We had fun. I managed to recoup my money from all bounced checks but two; one was a relative of a friend and the other a relative of a policeman. What frosts me is Mike Dida, that salesman, never paid me for the mens' stadium coats he took on consignment and sold. I called and wrote, but no money. Another store owner who sold some for me in Midtown paid me. If that's friends, who needs enemies, right?"

"That's retail for you!" Angela's famous words had often soothed me. We had also been drawn together while, at slow business periods, we listened to the radio to a favorite religious program. That boosted our morale when low.

That phrase covered a multitude of whatevers, I deducted, and would flit through my mind forever when shopping, I supposed. Remnants also took on a different meaning, not just odd pieces at the end of a bolt of cloth, as I tended to view them. A stark, somber look pervaded my lovely place of free enterprise, with its disorder, empty shelves, and banners of *doom*.

Ending a Dream

"Row, row, row your boat," (I did), "Gently down the stream," (I did), "Merrily, merrily, merrily, Life is but a DREAM!"

There was plenty of time to chat on the phone to anyone, as I remained to finish parting details. I told Angela, "All clothes are listed and packed in boxes now; tables distributed, wagons sold, and the mission comes for shelves and racks soon for its store. I've been busy contacting utilities for shutoff times and cleaning up the back room junk, too. The down jackets and toddlers' snowsuits were the last things sold last week. What happened to Mickey?

"Well, he had to cool his heels in jail a while, but he's been free on bond now. I called the prosecutor's office and was told the case is dismissed. Fingerprints on the cash register were lost, so there's no conclusive evidence either way. He was not likely to be convicted on such slim evidence as my identifying him. They're just completing the paperwork. He's *free*. Yes, isn't that a way to go. I don't think he'll bother me; at least we're closed so he can't walk in, though he may know where I live. I suppose that's why some victims don't prosecute. I was informed by the prosecutor, 'He's not likely to; if anything happened to you, we'd know who did it.' Great! I think he's dumb, but not that dumb, with his criminal record and probation. Incidentally, Alexandra is moving to that Lawton store soon. I'm glad. Will keep in touch, my dear."

Sitting around by myself, I could almost hear my remaining occupants discuss their futures...

"Elsie, my window is barren and I'm not visible behind this Going Out of Business banner. People squint past me to see what's left in this long, dark hole..."

"I know, Alexandra, and I feel I'm just waiting my life away. Glad you are moved here by me. I get it, your outfit has to be packed. Didn't want you on display in your nature suit, I'll bet. You're not cold with the heat off?"

"No, no one bought me so I'm leaving town soon for Lawton, dressed in some old rag. I shouldn't travel like this in my new owner's hatchback, you know. And you?"

"I leave when Charles takes boxes to keep. Here come the men from the mission. Are you embarrassed like that?"

"Not really. Oh, here's my *black* dress. Appropriate color for the occasion, and my new owner. I'll miss you."

"Alexandra, don't be sad, it's the end of a dream."

A True Sequel

"If anything happens to you, we'll know who did it."

I remembered those last words of the prosecutor to me when my case against Mickey was dismissed. How do I prevent *anything* from happening, besides keeping my doors locked? Forever? But then, why would he want me?

Mickey, the drugged thief I encountered alone in my clothing store two-

and-a-half years before had changed my life in many ways. I was beginning to forget the details of the painful assault and robbery: his tying my wrists and ankles with my vacuum cord while I lay on the floor and taking all the cash from my purse and cash register.

However, I couldn't forget Mickey. For over two years, the pelvic injury from his assault pained me most of the time. I finally developed a limp and griped silently, you are literally a pain in the buttocks! I considered consulting a nerve specialist. Even the memory of his bug eyes popped into my mind anytime; after all, I had seen him four times, maybe five.

The fifth I considered likely when during the summer after I closed my store, he strode past me near a lake where Lisa, her son, and I rested. He wore cutoffs and had a bedroll strapped to his neck. My heart stopped. Was he there, many miles from his town, to find me? He didn't see me. As other crime victims have said, "One is never the same again." I had deep suspicions toward strange young men, especially if they came into my home as handymen or salesmen. They made me alert.

Then on Friday morning in June I answered my phone. "Is Sara there?" asked an unfamiliar, muffled voice of either a man or woman.

"Speaking!" The caller *hung* up. I analyzed. Why not talk to me when it is me. Who wants to know where I *live?* Only *Mickey!* Now I'm *found!* He can trace me anywhere! No! Not that suspense again. Numb all over, I phoned Lisa, who soothed, "You can't be sure. Lock your doors, though!"

I told my next door neighbor. "If you see anything unusual, call the police. I had a suspicious phone call."

On Monday morning, I met a brown car a couple of blocks from my home, driven by a young man wearing a cap and black sunglasses, with shoulder length hair; Mickey's features evident. He didn't look at me, but my nerves tingled. From my rearview mirror, I observed him turn onto my road. I dreaded going home after my meeting, worried he'd be hiding somewhere. He was not.

That evening, I asked my neighbor, "Did you see a light brown car come up the road to our house? About ten o'clock this morning?"

"Yeah, I was working in the front yard. I saw a young guy turn around before your house."

"Well, I think the thief from my store is after me."

"That's awful! Are you sure it's him?"

"Yes, I've seen him enough! I need his license number checked, but I can't tell the police; he hasn't done anything, yet."

Checking Mickey's address revealed he lived forty miles away, in Lisa's town. I asked her, "Will you drive by for his license number. You live closer? I'm trying to think like a detective. Your dad said he'd hire one if I want him to, but not yet."

The next Monday, the phone rang. "Hello!" Silence! I immediately hung up, shaking. He's checking to see if I'm home or not! I felt helpless and lonely. I can't even pray. What next? He's had a breaking and entering offense. Calmed with religious music on the stereo, I remembered how David's music soothed King Saul in the Bible.

During the next week, while dusting near the front part of the house, I noticed an old blue car drive by, with two men in the front seat. But instead they stopped, backed into a spot to face my house from a short distance, then parked to wait. One looked like Mickey, without the hat. Again he wore the large dark shades; likely still on drugs. Confident I was not visible, I remained between the drapes. They talked and watched my house about twenty minutes.

I thought, They're casing! I feel so vulnerable! Can they get in?

Suddenly the unkempt driver started the engine, turned around, and drove down a dead-end street nearby. Are his friends so close? But I can't call the police. They can harass me again.

After that, I was cautious when I worked in my flower gardens, ready to dash for the house. The pressure mounted. If God allowed it once, why not again? I must surrender all. Finally, both Lisa and I, separately, noticed Mickey's brown car parked before his apartment address. That proved it was him. I was relived; I suspected some people thought I was becoming paranoid. The suspense was killing me.

Sally, another daughter, suggested, "Mom, this can't go on forever. You should report him. Or get the upper hand by writing him-let him know you saw him." She lived in another town but pictured my vulnerability when home alone.

"Sally, I never thought of that! Do you think it's safe? He might get angry and harm me, especially if he's on drugs. I felt he had another chance from God when his fingerprints were lost. I'll write a rough draft and call you. Thank you!"

The letter went something like this:

"Dear Mickey, how are you doing? I've seen you around. When our case was dismissed because your fingerprints were lost, I thought God was giving you another chance to do something with your life. He loves you, you know, and has a plan for your life. You are young yet and can change your way of life, but you need help. He will, if you ask Him. You will *live forever*, with Christ or without Him, so ask Him to forgive you and start over. You need goals; you must make the decision. I care. Sincerely, Sara."

I read it to Lisa and Sally, who said, "Wait twenty-four hours, pray about it. Call your pastor." They also prayed. I typed it and sent it without my last name or return address. I decided, if that isn't his address, the letter will be dumped. But he'll know I'm on to him, if it is.

For some reason, Charles decided to take a vacation the next week. I told him about the letter and that I was glad to leave town. He said, "Well, you can't be a prisoner in your own house, I know, but that's a police matter."

"I'll call the police if Mickey phones or comes around again! I'm sure they aren't proud of their losing fingerprints. I had to do something–for my sanity."

That evening as I prepared for bed, something was not the same. Now free from fear, I felt free from my pelvic pain. "I don't need pills–my limp is gone! My knee doesn't buckle! I'm *healed*! Thank God!"

And Mickey stopped the harassment–his car was gone. However, as time passed, symptoms of post-trauma syndrome occurred, but religious counseling relieved much of it. Though the dream was an adventure to remember, of the results, I know, "This, too, shall pass."